NEW JERSEY'S COLONIAL ARCHITECTURE

TOLD IN 100 BUILDINGS

DAVID VEASEY

FONTHILL

The William Faden map of The Province of New Jersey, published in London December 1, 1777, based on a survey made in 1769.

Contents

Acknowledgments

A book of this sort involving multiple historic properties across the entire state of New Jersey required the assistance and support of a number of people. Needless to say any mistakes or omissions are my fault. I especially want to thank Bob Craig of the DEP's Historic Preservation Office who aided me above and beyond the call of duty. I also want to thank Andrea Tingey of the Historic Preservation Office, and Joe Ross for showing me the Deerfield Presbyterian Church and other sites in Cumberland County. I also want to thank Katherine Craig at Boxwood Hall; Bob Sands, director at the Trent House; Janet Strom of the Bergen County Division of Cultural and Historic Affairs. I also want to thank the Ralston Historical Society and Pat and Mary at the Miller-Cory House in Westfield; Donald Sherblom at the Vought House, and Robert Francois president of the Millville Historical Society. The book is dedicated to my wife Dorothy who visited innumerable colonial buildings in our trekking around the state.

Fonthill Media LLC
www.fonthillmedia.com
office@fonthillmedia.com

First published in the United States of America 2014

Copyright © David Veasey 2014

ISBN 978-1-62545-047-0

B+T 24.95 11/14

Typeset in Mrs Eaves XL Serif Narrow
Printed and bound in England

Introduction

Every type of American architecture exits in New Jersey, except Spanish Colonial. New Jersey has the most varied colonial architecture in the nation because it was settled by the most diverse people compared to all other colonies, with the possible exception of New York City. A substantial number of buildings remain from our colonial past, ranging from mansions to farmhouse to urban row houses, to taverns, churches, forges, schools, stores, a lighthouse, and even a law office.

The Colonial Period in New Jersey lasted from 1636, with the first Dutch settlers in what is now Jersey City, to the signing of the Treaty of Paris in September 3, 1783, officially ending the Revolutionary War with Britain recognizing American independence.

Every county is represented in the book by at least one building. The 100 buildings or complex of buildings listed together are under a variety of ownership, including the National Park Service, NJ Division of Parks & Forestry, historical societies, county and municipal governments, as well as private individuals.

The 100 buildings were selected to represent a broad cross section of colonial New Jersey life and were drawn from the Historic American Building Survey (HABS) or the National Register of Historic Places. HABS is one of the alphabet relief agencies set up by President Franklin D. Roosevelt in 1933 during the Great Depression to hire unemployed architects, draftsmen, and photographers to document America's noted and ordinary buildings, a resume, if you will, of our architectural heritage. HABS remains a collaborative effort among the American Institute of Architects, National Park Service (NPS), and Library of Congress. Its drawings, photographs, and building narratives are housed within the Prints and Photographs Division of the Library of Congress. In the text accompanying each photograph, HABS is used instead of spelling out Historical American Building Survey each time it is cited.

The National Register of Historic Places and its companion National Historic Landmarks are National Park Service programs created in 1966 designed to list properties worthy of preservation. The National Register website defines their mission as "part of a national program to coordinate and support public and private efforts to identify, evaluate, and protect America's historic and archeological resources." New Jersey has more than 1,600 sites listed on the National Register of Historic Places. In the photo captions when citing the nominating petition for the National Register of Historic Places, I simply use Nominating Petition as a shortened citation.

National Historic Landmarks are buildings, sites or objects that have been vetted by the National Park Service and approved by the Secretary of the Interior as nationally significant in American history or culture. They must first be listed on the National Register of Historic Places before they can be nominated for National Historic Landmark designation. New Jersey has fifty-seven national landmarks, with fifteen of them from our Colonial Period. All colonial buildings are included except the Hermitage of Hohokus because it is been extensively altered beyond recognition from the original colonial structure. * Denotes building that is part of a complex.

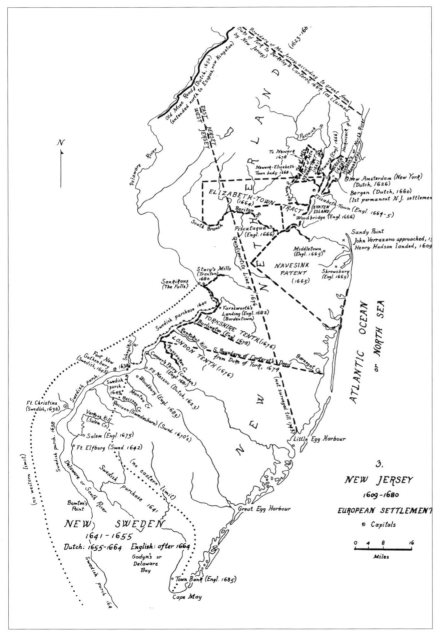

3.

NEW JERSEY
1609-1680

EUROPEAN SETTLEMENT

⊙ Capitals

0 4 8   16
Miles

A map of New Jersey showing European settlement 1609–1680. The symbol ° on the map indicates a regional capital.

European Roots Of New Jersey Buildings

New Jersey's colonial architecture reflected the diverse lands its early settlers came from, for in all cases those immigrants tried to duplicate the houses and churches of the lands they left behind. They built what they knew and had a mental image of what a house, church, or tavern should look like. All the other colonies, with the exception of New York City, were settled by relatively homogenous people with basically similar architectural styles.

The first European settlers in New Jersey were the Dutch, who crossed the Hudson River in 1636, a few years after their 1626 purchase and settlement on Manhattan Island. Two houses were built in what is now Jersey City. The would-be colony had trouble with the Indians and until they were defeated, immigration halted resuming in 1658. The first New Jersey town, which was Bergen, was established in 1660 in what is now Jersey City Heights. Over time, the Dutch settled all of Bergen County and parts of today's Essex, Morris, Passaic, and Somerset counties.

At the other end of New Jersey, Swedish colonists arrived in lower Delaware Bay on the ship *Kalmar Nyckel* in 1638, in what in time would become Wilmington, Delaware. The venture was sponsored by the New Sweden Company, modeled after the Dutch West Indies Company. Swedish settlers, including many Finns and others, began crossing the Delaware Bay and river into New Jersey. By 1643 the Swedes had built Fort Nya Elfsborg in what is today's Salem County, but its exact location has never been determined. These early settlers are remembered in the town names that still remain in Salem and Cumberland counties, such as Swedesboro, Finns Point, Eisinboro, Mullica Hills, the latter two are named after places in Sweden

Meanwhile, to the north in New England there was a major migration of Puritans from England in waves from 1629 to 1641, a period just preceding the English Civil Wars. These Puritans mostly hailed from the East Anglia section of England, which is the large peninsula that bulges into the North Sea, and whose heartlands are the counties of Suffolk and Norfolk.

There is much confusion among Americans between the Pilgrims who settled Plymouth Colony and the Puritans who settled Massachusetts Bay Colony. The Pilgrims were religious extremists-separatist who came from the lower orders of society, small farmers, laborers, and lesser artisans who wanted to establish their version of heaven on earth. While the Puritans came from the same background as those who later ruled England under Sir Oliver Cromwell and the Roundheads (Puritans). That is a middle class businessman, landowners, successful artisans, who migrated in family groups.

Some of these original settlers and their descendants in search of more and better farmland than New England's rocky terrain moved from Massachusetts Bay Colony to Long Island. In 1664 the Long Island Puritans were granted the right to settle in New Jersey, creating their first settlement in Elizabethtown that same year. The English settlement at present-day Elizabeth in 1664 is considered the beginning of New Jersey thus making the year 2014 the state's 350th birthday.

In quick succession these New England and Long Island Puritans bought land and created Middletown and Shrewsbury in 1665, Newark, Piscataway, and Woodbridge in 1666. In the 1680s Cape May also had its first settlements, mostly by whalers and farmers from Long Island, Connecticut, and Massachusetts Bay Colony.

About a decade after the Puritan settlements of Northern New Jersey, Quakers—The Society of Friends—began to emigrate in two distinct movements, first, in 1675 from London and nearby counties to Salem, founded by John Fenwick. The Quakers settled in New Jersey before they did in William Penn's Philadelphia, a fact often overlooked by historians who talk about the Quaker migration to Philadelphia. By and large the Quaker emigrants were skilled artisans, tradesmen, along with some gentlemen.

The second movement of Quakers took place two years later, when Quakers from England's north Midlands, counties of Lancashire, Yorkshire, and Nottinghamshire moved to Burlington in 1678. After 1682 the Quaker migration was diverted to William Penn's Philadelphia.

The next major group of settlers were Scots and Scots–Irish, mainly Presbyterians, who moved from Scotland and Northern Ireland in the 1680s, encouraged by Scottish grant holders in East Jersey. By 1683, they had settled in Perth Amboy.

Germans began arriving in New Jersey in the early eighteenth century, mostly from the Palatine area of Germany, rural villages in the Rhine River Valley centered on today's Koblenz, with Frankfurt the nearest large city. The story of the first German arrivals, which may be apocryphal, is that in 1707 a vessel with refugees from the Palatine bound for New York was forced off course by a raging Atlantic storm to the Delaware Capes. The ship sought refuge in Delaware Bay and sailed up river to Philadelphia. Many Germans stayed with the original plan and went overland across New Jersey to New York City, while some settled en route in Hunterdon and Morris counties.

In the next ten years many more Germans came into New Jersey, via stays in England before landing in Philadelphia. Because people migrate into regions where they have relations or where a number of their fellow countrymen lived, settlement patterns are not arbitrary but follow fixed paths. Those paths led into what is now Sussex and Somerset counties, in addition to the initial settlements in Hunterdon and part of Morris counties. In the 1750s, additional Germans arrived from Bethlehem, Pennsylvania to create the Moravian settlement in Hope, Warren County.

In 1745, New Jersey's population was 61,403 and by 1784 that had grown to 149,435 (Brush p. 17).

The map on page 6 shows the early settlement pattern of both East and West Jersey. Note the various land grants and also the East Jersey and West Jersey dividing line.

Division of East & West Jersey

New Jersey's early colonial history is complicated. The division of the colony into East and West Jersey began with the Dutch defeat in the Third Anglo-Dutch War in September 1664. The Dutch were forced to turn over New Amsterdam and their New Jersey possessions to the English. Just a couple of years earlier, Charles II had been restored to the English crown following the turmoil after the death of Oliver Cromwell in 1658.

In the simplest terms, the English Civil War took place between 1642 and 1651 pitting Royalist, who believed in the absolute power of the king, against supporters of Parliament who wanted to curb the king's power. The army behind Kings Charles I and II were known as Cavaliers, while the forces fighting for Parliament where called Roundheads. After his restoration to the English throne, Charles II in 1664 granted lands in New Jersey to his brother James, Duke of York, who in turn sold his lands to George Carteret and John, Lord Berkeley.

However, the British expeditionary force that had defeated the Dutch brought their own governor with them to rule the conquered territories. He was Colonel Richard Nichols. Before the Dutch defeat, Long Island Puritans had been negotiating to move to New Jersey. After the Dutch surrendered all their lands to the British, Col. Nichols immediately gave permission for the Puritans to enter New Jersey. In October 1664 Daniel Denton, John Bailey, and Luke Watson bought land from the Indians in New Jersey and began the Puritan migration.

Meanwhile, John, Lord Berkeley, and Carteret both sold their land grants to a subset of proprietors. Berkeley's lands would become West Jersey and Carteret's claim would be East Jersey. This act of sub division to still more proprietors, especially in East Jersey, would lead to centuries of court battles over land claims and other land ownership issues, with the last issue only settled in 1998.

Selling to the subset of Proprietors also led to immediate controversy with the groups Col. Nichols had granted land to in East Jersey. In West Jersey, Berkeley sold his land to only four sub-proprietors led by Quakers William Penn and John Fenwick, and there was little land ownership controversy. The early divisions of East and West Jersey have consequences even today. East Jersey, basically North Jersey, and West Jersey, today's South Jersey, was divided along what is today called Province Line Road that begins in Little Egg Harbor and cuts diagonally across the state to Sussex County. See map on page 6.

In 1703 the proprietary colonies of East Jersey and West Jersey were united as the Royal Province of New Jersey. Although the Colony was unified separate capitals were maintained in Burlington for West Jersey and Perth Amboy for East Jersey. The Royal Governor's house in Perth Amboy still stands (see page 48). It was not until 1790 that Trenton became the state capital.

Building Techniques

Although colonial New Jersey had diverse architectural styles they shared many of the same basic construction techniques and tools. All buildings, whether wood, brick, or stone had an internal framing system, which varied by architectural style. The Dutch framing technique was called anchor bent framing, which consisted of heavy timbers formed in an H shape. This technique comes from medieval barn construction in The Netherlands and neighboring Germany. The timbers were assembled on the ground and then raised into place. One architectural historian described the constructions as: "the heavy timbers form an H-shaped bent with the crossbar at the attic floor, and the bents are spaced approximately four feet apart for the length of the house. The roof was then attached at the plate on the upright legs, not at the attic level as in English one, or one and a half story houses. It is this structural system that gives most Dutch houses...their distinctive high-shouldered look" (Foster, p. 41) with extra wall height compared to English house construction.

The froe is a wedged-shaped cleaving tool.

Wood-frame houses were sheathed in planks or by shingles or shakes, which came in a variety of styles and sizes. Technically, a shake was hand-spilt wood siding, while a shingle was milled, although in colonial New Jersey the terms seem to be used interchangeably. The planks used in siding a house were called clapboards or occasionally weatherboards.

The tools used to make clapboards were saws, broadaxes, and adzs, a finishing axe. To make shakes and shingles another tool called a froe was used. The froe, shown on the left, was a key tool in making shakes and shingles. The hatchet like blade is placed in the wood to be split, at the thickness wanted. The handle is held in a vertical position with the left hand while the right hand wields a wooden froe mallet striking the back of the horizontal blade splitting the wood into the right thickness and length for the size of shake or shingle desired. With these pre-industrial tools a frame house could readily be built.

Bricks, another major colonial building material, were faced in a variety of patterns. The most common were Flemish bond, English bond, and common bond. In Flemish bond the stretcher, that is the brick lengthwise, is alternated with the brick faced end out or header, so it is alternate header and stretcher in the same row. In English bond rows are alternately headers and stretchers, while in common bond all the bricks are placed as stretchers. Of course, using headers and stretchers in various colors and arrangements can create ornate brick patterns.

A gable end.   A house with a gambrel style of roof.

The roofs of buildings are often keys to their style. During the Colonial Era in New Jersey there were three basic roof styles. The gambrel roof, which has two slopes, as shown above. Gambrel roofs are often thought of as typically Dutch although English construction and other architectural styles also used them. Many Dutch buildings do not use gambrel roofs, but have traditional gable ends. The gable roof, shown left above, is the triangular end of an exterior wall where it meets the roof. A hipped roof, rare in Colonial New Jersey, is defined as a roof that slopes upward on four sides of the exterior walls and is joined together at their apex or top of the house.

Architectural Styles

In most cases, architectural styles will be noted in the captions for the 100 buildings. Although a couple of different styles will be discussed briefly below. The Swedes and Finns, who had arrived in New Jersey by 1640, main architectural contribution was the log cabin. Contrary to what many history books say, early buildings in New Jersey and the other colonies were made of wood frame with cedar shakes and were not log cabins. For example, many New Jersey church histories talk about how their first church was made of logs, certainly not true because framing techniques were well known and used in their homeland. The wood frame was more than likely covered by shakes or shingles. That is why the froe was an important colonial tool. It was easy to make shingles with it, probably just as easy as notching logs with an axe for a log cabin. The Swedish log cabin, a 1750s version is shown on the next page, made its appearance in 1638 in what is now Wilmington, Delaware. A few years later Swedes and Finns had migrated across the river into New Jersey. Sweden was a heavily forested country and building houses of logs was a long-standing vernacular building tradition. It was from this woodsmen background that the early Swedish settlers to New Jersey brought their traditional building styles.

A Swedish log cabin is made of round or squared away logs, either with or without bark, with notched ends protruding. To fit logs together different notching systems are used, representing different ethnic groups such as Finns versus Swedes. Germans also made log cabins when they settled in rural Pennsylvania, but they could have learned these techniques from the Swedes in the Delaware valley or they could have learned about them in Switzerland, which also used log construction. It is uncertain. What is certain is that the log cabin became

A Swedish log cabin from the 1750s.

the home of choice for Scots-Irish pushing into frontier lands beyond the first ridge of the Appalachian Mountains. The log cabin became the symbol of the frontier as it advanced ever westward—and the Swedish log cabin became the American log cabin.

The frame house that became popular in the mid-1700s was basically a main or core house with an addition, known as a block and wing. This basic house is called a stack house in South Jersey, so named by a Philadelphia architect in the 1980s. In North Jersey this basic house is called an East Jersey Cottage, so named by Princeton University Professor Thomas J. Wertenbaker in the 1960s. Whatever you want to call it, it was a combination of New England and Dutch framing, with additions made to the side in the Dutch manner, as opposed to the English style of adding one room behind another. They were one story with a loft, with small window panes. The typical house was 45 feet wide by 18 feet deep with a chimney at either end.

Church Architecture

The Great London fire of September 1666 also had an impact on Colonial New Jersey. The fire gutted central London destroying 13,200 houses, 87 parish churches, and St Paul's cathedral as well as many government buildings. Christopher Wren, who was responsible for designing 51 London churches after the fire, had only become an architect a couple of years earlier. Prior to that he taught astronomy and mathematics at Oxford University.

The Wren-designed parish church of St. Stephen, Walbrook, London, 1678.

In 1669 Wren was appointed King's Surveyor of Works, a job that undoubtedly aided him in being responsible for rebuilding numerous churches. His rectangular churches, with a formal porch entry or portico, were built in a distinctive style of tower and steeple, with Georgian influences. It was a break from medieval churches. This style became popular in America in the late 1700s. It was transferred to this country as church builders became familiar with Wren's drawings or through pattern books. Other church builders may have gotten their ideas second-hand based on American churches, such as Old North Church in Boston. The Shrewsbury Episcopal Church (page 93) the Dutch Reformed Church in Hackensack (page 21) are all Wren-inspired buildings. The other distinctive style of New Jersey churches, from the late 1600s onwards to the American Revolution, was the meetinghouse style, a building that almost looks secular. Meetinghouse-style churches were a reaction to the ornate Catholic churches of Europe and to the Anglican churches of England. They were designed to reflect the plain life style of their congregations. Many of the meetinghouse churches were built in a Georgian style.

Georgian Style

Georgian style, named after the four British King Georges who ruled from 1714 to 1830, is both a time period and architectural style. Colonial architecture becomes a bit more complicated. Colonial is a time period, but has also evolved into an architectural style. Although only using colonial as a time period has support among architectural historians. However, the National Park Service's National Register of Historic Places uses Colonial as a building style. The successor to Colonial style is Georgian architecture, which is an updated English renaissance style or one that takes many elements of classical Greek and Roman architecture into its design.

Renaissance architecture developed in Florence, Italy. Art historians said it began with Brunelleschi's dome for the Florence Cathedral in 1418. Over the next two plus centuries, Renaissance architecture was found throughout Europe, coming last to England. The first professional British architect, Inigo Jones, is largely responsible for introducing England to the classical style of building. He was a theater set designer before evolving into an architect. He designed a number of British buildings, including Banqueting Hall and Queen's House, based on the work of Andrea Palladio, an Italian architect who lived in the late 1500s. Jones, incidentally, was the King's Surveyor of Works, a job Christopher Wren held 50 years later. Italian architect Palladio studied the buildings and monuments of ancient Rome and applied their classical style, which has been defined as "propriety, order, and proportion" (Tavernor, p. 8) to his building. Most of Palladio's buildings were in Northern Italy with a number of important buildings in Venice and Vicenza. Some have called Palladio the greatest architect who ever lived.

It is easy to see the relationship between the two buildings, shown on page 14; both are ordered, balanced, with restrained use of pilasters and feature tall windows. Queens House is closer to our ideal of a large-scale Georgian building. The English upper classes began building in the Jones style with its formal, symmetrical design. Windows and doors are placed in balance, not in an irregular pattern to meet the needs of an indoor room, the way medieval architecture does. Georgian homes had a central hall with rooms accessed off the central hall. America's coastal colonial elite followed the customs and architectural styles of the British upper classes.

Palladio's Palazzo Barbaran da Porto, in Vicenza, 1580.

Inigo Jones' Queens House in Greenwich, 1616.

The two mansions below are good examples of American Georgian architecture, with balanced, symmetrical façades and restrained decoration. The Georgian style came to America by British immigrant builders, by architectural drawings, and by pattern books that showed in detail how to build in the Georgian style. The change from a Colonial style house, with its more haphazard arrangement of doors and windows, to reflect the needs of the interior rooms, rather than reflecting an exterior design did not happen all at once. The Georgian style was popular and led to the Federal style, widely built after the end of the Revolutionary War to become the architecture of choice for a new nation.

The Ogden-Belcher Mansion, Elizabeth, 1742.

The Ford Mansion, Morristown, 1772.

New Jersey Colonial Architecture Told in 100 Buildings

New Jersey celebrates its 350th birthday in 2014 marking the official beginning of the first English settlement in Elizabethtown in 1664. This book is an informal guide to New Jersey's rich colonial heritage and aims to foster appreciation for buildings that have survived 250 years or more and to motivate all citizens to become involved with historic preservation. The book is organized roughly north to south, moving west to east. Most of the caption text comes from three sources: The Historical American Building Survey, nominating petitions for the National Register of Historic Places, and from studies and reports in the New Jersey Historic Sites Inventory, housed in the Preservation Office of the Department of Environmental Protection in Trenton. Any other books cited are noted by the author's last name and page number in the text, with a full reference in the bibliography.

Van Wagenen House, Jersey City

This Dutch farmhouse was built in what is now Jersey City Heights in the area of the first Dutch settlements in New Jersey. The main section of the house dates from the 1740s; the wing was added in the 1820s. The original building is an eight-room fieldstone and brick house, with a gable roof. The wing was built of the same material. It does not look like our image of a New Jersey Dutch farmhouse, which is a sandstone house of one-and- a -half stories, a gambrel roof, with overhanging eaves. The book will show the variety of Dutch architecture in the state. The property was conveyed to Garet Garretson by Governor Philip Carteret in 1688. Garretson for unknown reasons changed his name to Van Wagenen after his hometown in the Netherlands, Wageningen. The original farm was about 100 acres and included an apple orchard and a cider press, hence the alternate name as the Apple Tree House. It is one of the oldest houses in Hudson County and has just been renovated by the city. During the Revolutionary War, the house was said to have been used as a vantage point to spy on Loyalist New York City clearly visible across the Hudson River. The Van Wagenen family and its descendants by marriage owned the property for 279 years, until April 1947. After several owners and in deteriorating condition the county bought the house in 1994.

John Branford House, Wyckoff

One of the most attractive colonial houses in the state was built in stages between 1742 and 1776. The Dutch house shows progression from the earliest small structure on the left, built about 1742, to the largest section of the house, on the right, built in 1776 at the time of the Revolutionary War. The house mirrors the growth of Bergen County from relatively modest beginning to a settled affluent community by 1776. The builder was Barent Van Horn for the Ackerman Family. The house was sold to the Branford family in the 1870s. The 1742 house was expanded over the years to meet growing family needs. The main house was built of dressed sandstone on two walls, the other two are mixed rubble stone, that is fieldstones or quarried rock roughly finished, while dressed stone has been made into a standard, smooth size. Inside, the smallest building is used as a kitchen while the intermediate structure as a dining room, while the latest addition is two rooms deep, with the front room used as a living room and the two rear rooms as bedrooms and storage. Those were the room uses when the house was the subject of an HABS study in 1939. The house is privately owned.

Peter Garreston House, Fair Lawn

With its graceful gambrel roof, curved eaves extending outward over a red sandstone side wall, and one-and- a -half stories high, it perfectly matches our image of what a New Jersey, or more specifically a Bergen County Dutch farmhouse should look like. The house was built in two sections, the wing or section without the columns was the original structure, built of local sandstone in 1720–1725. The section with the columns was built in 1800 of matching sandstone, both are one-and-a-half stories. The dormer windows were added in 1900. The house has a dining room, kitchen, and two parlors with fireplaces downstairs, and four rooms upstairs. The first Garreston—Gerrit Gerritsen or Garreston, spelling varies—(see page 16) of the family who would eventually occupy the house in Fair Lawn, arrived in East Jersey in 1660. The family came from Wageningen on the Rhine River in the Netherlands. It was his son, Peter, born in 1684 in today's Jersey City who moved to Fair Lawn in the early 1700s and built the original stone house and a forge. According to ledgers found on the property, Peter ran a store during the Revolutionary War selling to both sides. The property remained in the original owners family until the 1950s. The house is part of the Stone Houses of Bergen County thematic listing on the National Register of Historic Places. It is owned by the Bergen County Historical Society.

Von Steuben House, River Edge

In 1782, Congress voted $2,400 plus $300 per month for life to Major General Baron Von Steuben for his invaluable wartime service to the American Revolution. Von Steuben, who came to aid the Revolution from Germany, was made Inspector General of the Continental Army. He drilled and trained American troops in the art of European warfare while they were encamped at Valley Forge. New Jersey awarded him what is today called the Von Steuben House, built in 1695 by David Ackerman, a Dutch farmer. The house is one-and-a-half stories, sandstone, with gambrel wood-shingled roof. It was later sold to the Zabriskie family who lived in it for three generations. The house was doubled in size in 1757 and a gambrel roof replaced the earlier gable one. The original house was half as long and only two-thirds as deep as the present building. The first floor has five rooms, including a kitchen and parlor, while, the second floor has two rooms. Because of his Loyalist activities during the Revolutionary War, the state seized Zabriskie's home and land and later gave the property to Von Steuben, with the proviso he must live in the house. Von Steuben was living in New York and did not want to live in the New Jersey house. The state eventually agreed he could sell the house and receive the interest from the sale proceeds for the rest of his life. Von Steuben's aide-de-camp, Captain Benjamin Walker, bought the house for £1,500 in 1788. Three months later he sold property to John Zabriskie, so the Loyalist family regained their property. The house is owned by the Bergen County Historical Society.

Wortendyke Barn, Park Ridge

The Dutch barn is one of the few remaining of the hundreds, if not thousands, of barns that once dotted Bergen County's Dutch farmlands. The barn was built in 1770 on what was then a 460-acre farm, owned by Fredrick Wortendyke, whose Colonial Era farmhouse still stands across the street. The family settled here in 1735. In the Netherlands, where the barn design came from, many barns included family living quarters as warmth from animals augmented sometimes meager heating fireplaces. In Dutch New Jersey, New York, and Long Island barns were always separated from the farmhouse. The barn was made of local timber and wooden pegs were used instead of nails in the H-frame construction. Broader than it is deep, an historic marker explains, the structure is entirely supported by four H-frames tied with massive anchor beams. The barn's front and rear wagon doors were aligned permitting through access to the threshing floor, which had space for animal stalls on each side of the main floor. The barn is about 45 feet wide and 37 feet deep. It is now a museum owned by Bergen County Parks Department, which restored it in 1973. Until the county took it over the barn was used as a garage.

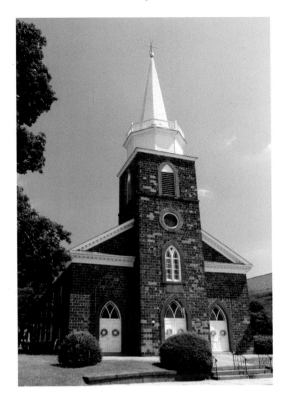

First Reformed Church, Hackensack

In the heart of Dutch Bergen County this building is slightly out of the Colonial Era, but its location, history—the congregation was founded in 1686—and its beautiful and historic style in the Christopher Wren tradition of tower and steeple, made its inclusion important. It was built in 1791 of dressed sandstone in a rectangular plan, with a pediment, gable roof, and central front tower. The HABS study of the church said: "Comparison with First Presbyterian Church in Elizabeth (1784) and Newark (1791) shows these notable examples of the Georgian style to have been the prototype of Dutch churches erected in Bergen County and elsewhere." During the Revolution, for the first time Dutchmen got to know English people in Newark and Elizabeth, along with their Georgian-style architecture. The churches in Elizabeth and Newark, in turn, were modeled after churches Christopher Wren built in London following the Great Fire. There were two previous Dutch Reform Churches on the Hackensack site, the first in 1696, the second in 1726, both were built as octagons. The octagon building layout was used by a number of Dutch Reform Churches inspired by the first Dutch protestant church built in 1595 at Williamstadt, Holland, which was octagon shaped. Church records from 1790 said the old church would be knocked down and on the same ground a new one would be built. The new church was to measure 48 feet deep by 60 feet wide with two second story-level galleries, all paid for by voluntary subscription. The church records go on to say, "the inside of the church shall be furnished with pews, without making any distinction between men's and women's pews." A total of £329 was subscribed by 135 persons pledging support. The church is still active.

Dey Mansion, Wayne

The mansion served as military headquarters for George Washington during July, October, and November 1780. Washington and about 4,000 soldiers arrived there on July 1, 1780, from their Morristown Encampment. Washington was marching north to link-up with Count Rochambeau and 6,000 French troops who had recently landed at Newport, Rhode Island. The house Washington stayed in was built by Dirck Dey in about 1740 on his 600-acre estate. The east wing or smaller structure attached to the main building was the original house. The larger section or today's main house was completed by Dey's son, Colonel Theunis Dey. The eight-room Georgian-style house is 52 feet long and 35 feet deep, and has a brick front, laid in Flemish bond. The end and rear walls are made of rubble stone; the mansion features dressed stonework around windows and door for decorative effect across the front of the house. The house has a gambrel roof. Dey was a carpenter and builder and third generation American of Dutch descent. He was active in politics as a Bergen County Freeholder (Passaic County was then part of Bergen County) and as a member of the New Jersey Assembly from 1748 to 1752. Dirck's son, Theunis Dey, was a Colonel in the Revolutionary War militia and also a member of the New Jersey Assembly and New Jersey Provincial Council. The house is owned by Passaic County.

Blacksmith Shop, Ringwood Manor State Park

Ringwood Manor was an early, important iron-making plantation with a blast furnace, forges, and blacksmith shops. The small, one-story fieldstone building, with a wood shingle roof, was one of the blacksmith shops; it was built in 1765. The difference between a blacksmith and a forge is one of degree. The forge was a larger scale operation and probably made more and different products. Blacksmiths made a variety of pans, kettles, cooking pots, axes, carpenters tools, coopers and tanner's tools, shovels, sheers, saws, and knives, for local consumption. Socially, a blacksmith ranked up there with a doctor and other community leaders. The Ringwood Manor blacksmith shop made some of the links for the chain that stretched across the Hudson River near West Point to stop British ships from sailing north on the river during the Revolutionary War. The present-day manor house, built in the early 1800s, absorbed the earlier house built in the mid-1740s when the site was being developed by the Ogden family into a major ironworks. By 1765 German immigrant Peter Hasenclever made Ringwood the center of his investor's London-based American Company, an iron-making and mining enterprise that included sites in New Jersey, New York, and Nova Scotia. In 1771, Robert Erskine replaced Hasenclever and managed this and two other principal iron-making complexes from his headquarters at Ringwood. During the Revolutionary War, Erskine was the Continental Army's first geographer and Surveyor General, who made more than 200 highly accurate maps. Ringwood was the beginning of the American and iron and steel industry. The site is part of Ringwood Manor State Park, which is a National Historic Landmark.

Worker Housing, West Milford

The two-family, double-entry rough-cut stone house was built in 1767 as workers lodging at Long Pond Iron Works. In colonial New Jersey workers, servants, and slave housing were generally built in the style and material commonly used in the area, and were not tumbledown shacks as often depicted. Long Pond Ironworks was established in 1766 by Peter Hasenclever, a German immigrant working for the London-based American Company. A year earlier the same company bought the Ringwood Ironworks (see page 23). Hasenclever managed the various iron making locales and activities from Ringwood Manor. To staff the New Jersey ironworks, Hasenclever brought more than 500 workers from Germany and England. Hansenclever's London investors were unhappy with his management and relieved him of his duties in 1769 and appointed Swiss iron-maker Johann Jacob to be in charge. Robert Erskine took over at Ringwood and Long Pond becoming ironmaster in 1771. In the Colonial Period the ironworks consisted of other worker housing, including a barracks for single men, a forge, a blast furnace, two blacksmith shops, a mill and related sluiceways and reservoir. The ironworks could produce 20 to 25 tons of pig iron a week. Long Pond is a translation of the Indian name for what is today Greenwood Lake. The technology transfer of German iron making and bringing in experienced German workers under Hasenclever had a strong impact on the development of the iron and steel industry in New Jersey over the next century. New Jersey was the nation's leading mining and iron producing area until after the Civil War when the industry shifted westwards in the 1870s and 1880s. Long Pond was in operation from 1767 to April 1882. The site is now managed by Ringwood Manor State Park.

Westbrook-Bell House, Sandyston Township

In the early 1700s, Johannes Westbrook built a low-level Dutch farmhouse in New Jersey's rugged northwest frontier country, where skirmishes with Indians were still common. The one-and-a-half story house was built in 1701 or 1725, depending on the source; it is fieldstone with clapboard gable ends. A 1967 HABS study said the L-shaped house was built in two different periods. The older and larger section was built in 1725 (or 1701) and the other section just before 1775. The house is 43 feet long by 23 feet wide. A cellar and tunnels underneath the house were built as protection against Indian attacks. The well-preserved exterior illustrates the variety in early Dutch farmhouses. The house is built just off the historic Old Mine Road, which was a series of interconnected roads that ran from the Delaware Water Gap to Kingston, New York on the Hudson River. There was a small Dutch community on lands bordering the Delaware River in early eighteenth century northern New Jersey who had come down along the Delaware River from New York State. In the case of Westbrook, he lived in Kingston, New York before moving to New Jersey. The Bell family married into the Westbrook family, hence the Westbrook-Bell name. The house remained in the family until 1972 when it was seized by the federal government as part of the Tocks Island Reservoir land grab for a reservoir that was never built. After the defeat of the Tocks Island Dam, the seized land became part of the Delaware Water Gap National Recreation Area. The National Park Service owns the house.

*Casper Shafer House, Stillwater Township

Casper Shafer moved to Stillwater in 1741, just three years after emigrating to Philadelphia from the Palatine region of Germany, which is centered on the Rhine River near present-day Koblenz. By 1743 Shafer had erected a wooden gristmill on the Paulinskill River. He also built a wooden frame house, the wing of the present house, probably two years earlier. The main stone house was built in 1750 and features stonework that was typical of German houses in colonial New Jersey, but it also shows the symmetrical influence of the Georgian style. The original house was moved from near the river and added as a wing to the main house, the porch was also added at a later date.

A number of other German families settled in Stillwater, most came from Philadelphia and southeast Pennsylvania. As Revolution brewed in 1775, Shafer became a member of Sussex County Committee of Safety and delegate to the New Jersey Provincial Assembly. Following the defeat of British and Hessians at the Battle of Saratoga in upstate New York in September and October 1777, thousands of Hessian prisoners were marched through Sussex County on their way to prisoner camps in Pennsylvania. A number escaped and Shafer and other German immigrants in Stillwater sheltered them because they were fellow Germans. A number of escaped Hessians stayed in the area after the war, becoming productive citizens. Shafer's original mill burned in the early 1790s and a 1796 replacement gristmill burned in 1844. The current mill is the 1844 mill. The mill and house are now owned by the state, but are not open to the public.

Shafer Slave House, Stillwater Township

Many people today are surprised to learn that New Jersey was a slave state, with most of the slaves held in Dutch and German settled areas of East Jersey. The Casper Shafer Slave House was built in 1780 around the corner from his own Stillwater house. Shafer owned about a dozen slaves, it is not known how many lived in this stone, three-story house. It was noted earlier that slave quarters were built in the same style and with the same materials as the prevailing vernacular architecture of the area. The slave house's most dominant feature is a porch on both the first and second floors that runs the length of the façade. The roof has brick chimneys at the gable ends. Today, the house has six rooms, including three bedrooms. Simply based on the sheer number of laws about slavery, it was an important aspect of early colonial economic life in New Jersey. The colonial laws included codes for slaves' behavior, the conditions they could be held, and other aspects of a slave's life. The early East Jersey proprietors promoted slavery to alleviate a perceived labor shortage. In general, in the Proprietary Colony (1664–1702) slaves were regarded by the law very much as were apprentices and servants. At the urgings of Quakers, New Jersey made slavery illegal in a number of steps beginning with a 1786 law banning the import or export of slaves. The law also said slavery should be curbed "in order that white labor may be protected" (Cooley, p. 31). Slavery was finally abolished in 1846. Slavery grew in New Jersey from 4,606 slaves in 1745, with a total population of 61,383 or 7.5 percent of the population enslaved. In 1790, well into statehood, there were 11,423 slaves in a general population of 184,139 or 6.2 percent enslaved (Cooley, p. 31).

Obdiah LaTourette Mill, Washington Township, Morris County

In the mid to late 1700s there were a number of mills along the South Branch of the Raritan River in what was then called Dutch Valley. After the initial Dutch settlement, Germans from Pennsylvania migrated across the Delaware River to this easternmost German settlement in New Jersey. The area changed its name to German Valley, and the name was changed once again during World War One to Long Valley. Today, Long Valley takes in most of what was German Valley, a slice of land about ten miles long and one to two miles wide in western Morris County. In 1750 Philip Weise, one of the original settlers of Long Valley, built a gristmill. The three-story wooden mill was originally powered by two water wheels, both were underneath the structure. The mill was operated for more than 125 years before being sold in the 1870s to Obdiah La Tourette. He expanded the mill, which remained in operation until the early 1940s. It was a mainstay of the local economy for almost 200 years. The mill has most of its 1870s equipment intact, it is now a museum owned by the Washington Township Land Trust.

Henry Doremus House, Montville Township

The house is locally famous as a place where George Washington and Alexander Hamilton stayed on June 24 and 25, 1780 following the Battle of Springfield. The house was on the main road between Morristown and West Point, a road used extensively during the Revolutionary War. The home's owner at the time of Washington's stay was Henry Doremus, a third generation New Jerseyan whose great grandfather Cornelius Doremus immigrated from the Netherlands. The house was built in 1760. The one-and-a-half story Dutch farmhouse is made of fieldstone, with upper clapboard gables, and two interior chimneys at either end. It was a comfortable four-room house, with two rooms on the ground floor, accessed by two exterior doors, one for each room. The upper half story had two rooms. A rear wood-frame kitchen was added in the 1770s. The family moved to the Montville area in 1708 from Paterson. Henry Doremus was a tanner who also owned a small farm of 62 acres. The Nominating Petition said: "Because of its lack of embellishment and the fact that plumbing, central heating, and electricity have never been introduced into the house, it maintains a convincing eighteenth century appearance despite some nineteenth century alterations of windows and doors. Although much worn, the original walls, woodwork, and floors retain an excellent degree of integrity." The house is owned by Montville Township.

Lebbeus Dod House, Mendham

The general public might have completely forgotten about Dod, an instrument and clock maker, except for an historic marker in front of his house. But his work lives on at the Metropolitan Museum of Art, where his parallel ruler with protractor and plotting scale is displayed in the American Decorative Arts section. The Dod family came to Mendham in 1745, when Lebbeus was a boy, from Guilford, Connecticut. The family was well-known as clock and instrument makers. Stephen Dod, father of Lebbeus Dod, built the wooden-frame house in about 1750. The house, with gable ends, is sheathed in gray shingles, and is in good condition for a wooden house more than 260 years old. During the Revolutionary War, Lebbeus Dod was an artillery captain in the Morris County Militia. At one point in the war, General Washington ordered that Dod be detached from active service to establish a musket repair service for the Continental Army on his farm. Repairing muskets and other small arms was a natural extension of his instrument and clock-making skills. Because of weapons repair operation, the British Army raided the Dod farm, but he escaped. Lebbeus Dod lived from 1739 to 1816. It is Lebbeus's instrument on display at New York's Metropolitan Museum. His family home is privately owned.

Black Horse Inn, Mendham

The Black Horse Inn, located in the center of Mendham, has been in continuous operation as a tavern since 1743. Today's upscale tavern and restaurant was founded by Ebenezer Byram in his farmhouse along a stagecoach route. It was built about 1740 initially as a farmhouse and was converted to a tavern by 1743. The inn's owner came to Mendham from Bridgewater, Massachusetts in approximately 1740. He was considered a wealthy and religious man. His son, Eliab, studied at Harvard College for the ministry, graduating in 1740. He was the first minister of Mendham's First Presbyterian Church also known as Hilltop Church. While the Black Horse Inn has been altered over the years, the center core of the building is close to its original look of two-and-a-half story wood frame with clapboard exterior. There was once a pair of exterior doors leading into the building, one to the tavern, and the other to the lodging section. The taproom door was removed in 1983 when the porch was enclosed. Taverns were important colonial social and meeting centers and the Black Horse Inn was also a polling place. From the beginning of both East and West Jersey taverns were required to be licensed. In England a distinction was made between and inn and a tavern. An inn was licensed to have overnight guests as well as serve food and drink, while a tavern could only serve food and drink. This legal distinction gradually fell away in New Jersey where tavern and inn came to be used interchangeably. Shortly after independence in 1784, New Jersey had 446 taverns.

Ralston Gristmill, Mendham

The attractive stone residence with an A-frame façade has an ageless quality and could have been built 10 to 100 years ago, but a stone marker below the white pediment extending from the roof, has 1732 carved into it. The mill was converted to a house in 1940. From its founding in 1732 until 1900 it was an import rural milling operation. The three-story fieldstone mill was built by John Logan on the North Branch of the Raritan River. During the Revolutionary War, Logan was a commissary for the Continental Army camped at nearby at Jockey Hollow. Tradition has it that Logan was paid in almost worthless Continental money for the flour he furnished the soldiers in the winters of 1777 and 1779. This form of non-payment forced Logan into bankruptcy after the War, belying a saying carved into one of the mill's interior beams that said, "flour is money." The mill was sold to his son-in-law John Ralston, a merchant from Pennsylvania, married to Margaret Logan. Ralston developed the mill into a rural industrial complex, establishing a sawmill, fulling mill, and running the gristmill. He also owned a store, worker housing, and a manor house. The workers' house is basically a Georgian structure, while the Manor House is considered an Adams style, which it was called in England or Federal style as it was called in the United States. The style evolved from the Georgian, but was more classically oriented following a renewed interest in ancient Rome prompted by the archaeological excavations taking place in Pompeii and Herculaneum. Ralston's mill, under different ownership, remained in business until 1900. The Ralston Mill is a private residence.

Ralston Manor House & Mill Worker Housing, Mendham

Top, Ralston Manor, was built in 1781 for John Ralston in a Federal style, with a gambrel roof and chimneys at either end. The Federal style was an outgrowth of Georgian, but with more emphasis on the vertical and being symmetrical. Below, the mill workers house was built in 1760 in a Georgian style just around the corner from the Manor House. It is not known how many workers lived in the house.

Ralston General Store, Mendham

The one-story general store was built about 1780 of wood frame with heavy clapboard sheathing. It served as the Ralston Mill office and also as a general store. A 1786 store inventory listed the following categories of items for sale: spices and liquors; tobacco; tools; chemicals; cloth and leather; personal accessories; clothing; house wares; hardware; and books. The store is now a museum owned by the Ralston Historical Society.

Wick House, Morris Township

The Wick property is famous as the site of the Continental Army's encampment in two separate winters in the Morristown area, those of 1777 and 1779. The one-and-a-half story wood frame house was built between 1746 and 1748 by Henry Wick. It is based on a New England house, a building style the Wicks brought with them when they moved from the Puritan settlement at Bridgehampton, Long Island to New Jersey in 1745. The farmhouse is shingles over frame in the front, and clapboards on the other sides. It has gable ends. It was expanded from an original single room to a second room on the other side of the chimney, thus the chimney is now in the center of the house. There are two rooms in the one-half story upper level. The Wick House was the subject of a 1930s HABS study; it was also extensively rehabilitated in the 1930s. Wick's prosperous 1,400-acre farm was first occupied by the Continental Army after Washington marched his troops to Morristown following victory at the Battle of Princeton, January 3, 1777. He chose Morristown and its outlying farms as his headquarters and soldiers' encampment because to the east the Watchung Mountains provided a barrier to any British advance that might come from New York City, only thirty miles away. Lookouts on the ridges could spot any enemy activity. Washington was in Morristown from January to May 1777. The second encampment, 1779–1780, was the worst winter in the eighteenth century. During this winter, General Arthur St. Clair made his headquarters at the Wick House while nearly 10,000 soldiers camped on Wick's and other nearby farms, in what is now the Jockey Hollow section of Morristown National Historic Park. The National Park Service owns the Wick House.

Wick House Pantry & Smokehouse, Morris Township

Storage rooms adjacent to early colonial kitchens went under a couple of different names depending on what was being stored, such as buttery (originally bottlery) for beer and ale; pantry, from the French pain, for bread and dry goods. Later, both pantry and buttery were used interchangeably and the pantry became an all-purpose kitchen storage room. The Wick House pantry was the coldest room in the house and was used to store food, drink, and cooking equipment. The smokehouse, behind the main house, was used to preserve chicken, beef, pork, and fish by first packing them in salt and then hanging them from rafters while a fire of wet hickory chips and logs burned for several days thus smoking and preserving the food. In the later Colonial Period it became fashionable to have smoke houses, small plaster-lined closets, built into the attic attached to an opening in the main chimney to vent the smoke.

Washington's Headquarters, Morristown

The Jacob Ford Mansion, George Washington's Morristown headquarters during the winter of 1779–1780, is one of the most important Colonial-Era buildings in America. It is an outstanding example of Georgian architecture. It was built of flushed-board siding, scored and painted white to look like masonry, with Palladian windows framing the entrance. The Ford home, like several other prominent New Jersey mansions, was built of wood, although brick was the usual material for grand homes. The 9,000 square feet structure was built between 1772 to 1774, on a slight knoll about a half-mile or so from Morristown center. It is two-and-a-half stories with chimneys at both gable ends. The first floor has a high-ceiled dining room, office, and reception rooms. The kitchen, as was the fashion in the day, was detached from the main house as a fire safety measure. The second floor consists of bedrooms. Jacob Ford, the home's owner and a local iron smelter operator, had died of pneumonia while on active militia duty. His widow allowed Washington and his staff to occupy most of the house, while the Ford family lived in two rooms on the first floor. A year earlier, Washington also had his headquarters in Morristown at Arnold Tavern on the town green. It was these two encampments and Washington's headquarters that led Morristown to call itself Military Capital of the American Revolution. The National Park Service took over responsibility for the house in 1933 from the Washington Association that had preserved the house after buying it in 1893. Morristown National Historic Park was the nation's first historic park; all the predecessors were natural wonders. It is second only to Mount Vernon for its number of Washington memorabilia. The Ford Mansion is a National Historic Landmark.

Cannonball House, Springfield

The Hutchings House, also known locally as Cannonball House, stands in tribute as one of only four buildings that survived the little-known Revolutionary War Battle of Springfield. The battle developed on June 23, 1780, while an American force of 1,500 soldiers under General Nathaniel Greene and Colonel Elias Dayton were blocking 5,000 British and Hessians soldiers *en route* to capture military stores at Morristown. The British felt they had to stop Washington's momentum and wanted to capture the military weapons and supplies at Morristown and trap the Continental Army at its Jockey Hollow encampment. The British were held in check as Americans troops slowly retreated from Springfield to Short Hills. The battle was considered a British defeat. In revenge, the British burned every building in Springfield, including the prominent Presbyterian Church, leaving only Cannonball House and three other buildings intact. The houses standing were those of Loyalists so it is believed Loyalists controlled the burning of the town. The cannonball, for which the house was named, lodged in the west wall during the battle. There is some controversy when the house was built, some sources said 1741, and other sources said it was built in 1770. Either way, the early Georgian-style house is wood frame with clapboard on three sides and shingles on the front. The two-story house is two rooms deep on each level, with a central hall giving access to all rooms. Most of the flooring is original, as is the east chimney. A kitchen wing was added to the rear of the house in the 1920s. The house is owned by the Springfield Historical Society.

Plume House, Newark

Offices for the House of Prayer, a Presbyterian Church, is the oldest building in Newark, built in 1726. The two-story brownstone, with a gable roof, was built for John Plume as a private home. The exterior has been changed from its original two-and-half-story profile with a gambrel roof. The house has ties to the Van Wagenen family in Jersey City (see page 16), as Plume's wife was Ann Van Wagenen. It was a private home until 1849 when it became the rectory for the Episcopal Church. The house is now used for church administrative offices. A footnote to the building's later history is that Rev. Hannibal Goodwin invented celluloid motion picture film here in 1867. Goodwin was rector of the House of Prayer from 1867 to 1887. He wanted to make a more durable film for stereopticons eventually created "a malleable, rollable, flexible film, which is the basis of motion picture in its various forms." said an historic marker in front of the building. The house is considered in peril because it is just a few feet from busy Interstate 280.

Liberty Hall, Union

The Governor William Livingston Mansion, also called Liberty Hall, was home to two prominent New Jersey families, the Livingstons and Keans, who produced senators, congressmen, governors, and other state officials for two centuries. The mansion was built from 1772–1773 for William Livingston, first governor of New Jersey. Livingston, originally from Albany, New York, was an attorney and active politically. He and his family moved to Liberty Hall in 1773. The initial wooden frame building was 83 feet in width, two stories high, with a gambrel roof and two flanking interior chimneys. The central section of the mansion had one-story wings attached to either side. The house has been extensively altered over the years, the rear of the mansion is now of Italianate design and a third floor has been added. The façade, except for the extra story, looks closest to the original building that Livingston lived in. Livingston served as governor from August 1776 until his death in July 1790. Except for an interlude from 1798 to 1811, the Livingston and later Kean families lived in Liberty Hall until 1995. The house was sold in 1798, and was regained by the two families when Peter Kean bought the home in 1811 in trust for his mother Susan Livingston. At that time women could not own property. Liberty Hall is a National Historic Landmark. It has been a house museum since 2000.

Boxwood Hall, Elizabeth

Elizabeth has three historic houses on one block, all less than 100 yards of each other on East Jersey Street. They are Belcher Mansion, Bonnell House, and Boudinot Mansion also called Boxwood Hall. The later was built about 1750. It was home to Elias Boudinot member of the Continental Congress and its president from 1782–1783. Boudinot was born in Philadelphia in 1740. Years later, he became a lawyer after studying under Rickard Stockton, (see page 73) whose sister he married in 1762. He lived in Elizabeth and commuted to his law practice in Newark, buying Boxwood Hall in 1772 from Samuel Woodruff, a wealthy merchant and later mayor of Elizabeth. During the Revolutionary War Boudinot was Commissary General of Prisoners. His final public post was Director of the U.S. Mint, a position he held from 1795 to 1805. On his appointment, Boudinot moved to Burlington near the Philadelphia mint. At that time he sold his mansion to Jonathan Dayton, a Revolutionary War hero. In 1805 Boudinot retired to study the bible and was one of the founders of the American Bible Society in 1816, which still exists in New York City. Boudinot lived at Boxwood Hall from 1772 to 1795. The 18-room mansion has been reduced to eight rooms as most of its surrounding property was sold. The two-story wood frame house, sheathed in shingles, has a gable roof with two inside end chimneys. The mansion is about 55 feet wide and 35 feet deep, with a center hall that extends through the house. The house was refurbished in 1942. Overall, what remains of the house is largely original. Boxwood Hall passed through several owners until a preservation society bought the house in 1939. It is a National Historic Landmark owned by the state.

Boxwood Hall Interiors

Top, Boxwood Hall dining room; bottom, bedroom of Elias Boudinot's wife, Hannah Stockton Boudinot; both rooms circa 1775.

Belcher-Ogden Mansion, Elizabeth

Jonathan Belcher was a failed Royal Governor of Massachusetts and New Hampshire, but was politically well connected as a friend of King George I, so he was given a second chance in politics and was appointed Governor of New Jersey. He was governor from 1747 until his death in 1757. Belcher hailed from a wealthy Cambridge, Massachusetts family. He was born on January 8, 1681, later graduated from Harvard College, and spent time in Great Britain where he met the future King George I, opening the door to his political career. He was appointed Governor of Massachusetts and New Hampshire simultaneous posts he held from 1729 to 1741. He was removed from office because of friction with powerful local opponents amid charges of bribery and theft. He was named Royal Governor of New Jersey in 1747. While governor, he was a strong supporter of what would become Princeton University, but declined the honor of having the college's main building named Belcher Hall. He suggested instead Nassau Hall, after King William III and the House of Nassau. During his tenure as Royal Governor Belcher lived at the home of John Ogden, built in 1742. It is uncertain whether Belcher rented the house or was simply given its use. The Ogden-Belcher mansion is a two-and-a-half story, Georgian-style brick structure. The front has different brickwork than the rest of the house, indicating that it was added to. The best explanation is the central part of the house was built in 1722 and added to in 1742 when Belcher moved in. After Belcher's death the house remained in the Ogden family, a prominent New Jersey family in their own right, until 1786. Today, the house is run by the Elizabethtown Historical Foundation.

Miller-Cory House, Westfield

The farmhouse is an excellent example of a dwelling that was common in New Jersey, known as 'Block and Wing,' where a main section (block) was built at one period, and later another section was added (wing) containing kitchen, bedroom, or any other room or two needed for a growing family. Houses like this one have also been described as East Jersey Cottages. Inside, is a two-room center hall with two corner fireplaces connected through a common chimney. The one-and-a-half story main house is wood frame, with clapboard exterior, it was built in 1740. The wing on the right side of the house was added as a kitchen in the late 1700s. The farmhouse has been little altered over the years and looks very much as it did when the Millers and Corys lived there. The home's first owner was Samuel Miller, who was born in 1718 in Elizabethtown. His great grandfather had moved from Long Island to Elizabeth, both grandfather and great-grandfather were associates of Elizabethtown and acquired land in Westfield. Land became available when 1,000-acre lots were appropriated among the original settlers in what was called the Clinker Lot Division of 1699–1700. Joseph Cory II bought the property at the end of the eighteenth century. He was a descendant of John Cory who was an early settler and came to Westfield about the same time as William Miller. An historic association owns the house.

Miller-Cory Interiors

Above, Miller Cory house kitchen, which has been slightly altered with a replacement fireplace, but otherwise the kitchen is authentic; first floor master bedroom, all floorboards and beams are original.

Robinson Plantation House, Clark

The Robinson house is one of the oldest buildings in New Jersey, built about 1690 for William Robinson, a surgeon who had emigrated from Scotland to East Jersey. The house has many medieval English features such as a steep roof, stepped in chimney, and casement windows with diamond patterns. The steep roof is a carry-over from the time when most roofs were made of thatch. The roofs were steep so that water would run off quickly and not pool and rot the thatch. The roof also has overhangs on the gable ends. Inside, the use of large internal framing beams, held together with wooden pegs, is considered a model of English heavy-beam construction. The winding staircase is the type that later was called Jersey Winders. The winding staircase was a space-saving technique and was not steep and narrow for defense the way medieval castles used narrow staircases that could be defended by one swordsman. The one-and-a-half story house is 21 feet deep by 31 feet wide. Dr. Robinson his wife and three children moved to what is now Clark Township in 1686 after he bought more than 700 acres along the Rahway River. Robinson was one of New Jersey Colony's first medical doctors. William Robinson died in 1693 and his son inherited the house. Five families have occupied the house since it was built. It was a private home until 1973, when an historical society acquired the house.

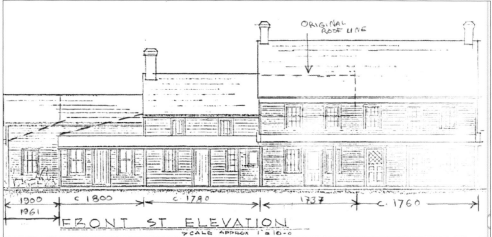

Stage House Inn, Scotch Plains

As the old real estate cliché goes location is everything. The Swift Sure Stage Line made the Stanberry Inn an important stop on its route from Philadelphia to Elizabeth via New Hope then across the Delaware River to Flemington, Somerville, Bound Brook, and right past the tavern in Scotch Plains to its destination in Elizabeth. The stagecoach road started as an Indian footpath, known as the Minisink Trail, evolved into the colonial-era York Road, and today is a busy county highway. The inn certainly chose the right road for its location because it has been in continuous business since 1737. It is two-and-half stories, wood frame construction, covered by clapboards. As the drawing shows, the inn was built in stages over the years to reach its current size. In the 1780 section, it is believed the innkeeper and his family lived in the full two-story house. Not much is known about Stanberry, the inn's owner, other than he came to Scotch Plains in 1689 and was the first deacon of the local Baptist church. Stanberry Inn's name was changed to Stage House Inn at an unknown date.

Royal Governor's Mansion, Perth Amboy

Proprietors of East Jersey wanted to enhance their capital city and also influence the Crown Colony government so they built a mansion for New Jersey's Royal Governors in Perth Amboy in 1762. It is the only colonial Royal Governor's house still standing. It is a brick three-and-a-half stories, on a raised basement, with gambrel roof, originally topped by a cupola, which has been removed. There is a decorative stone belt between the first and second stories; the brickwork is in Flemish and English bond. It is not recorded how many rooms the colonial mansion had, but after an 1809 addition converting it into a hotel there were 42 rooms. When the mansion was completed, it was first occupied by Frederick Smythe, Chief Justice of the New Jersey Colony. Royal Governor William Franklin, son of Benjamin Franklin, moved into the house in October 1774. On the eve of the Revolutionary War, Benjamin Franklin visited his son and tried but failed to convince him to support the Revolution. Shortly after the visit, he wrote a friend: "I am deserted by my only son." With the outbreak of War Franklin was placed under house arrest while his wife fled to New York City. During the war the house was used by the British Army. The Franklins left New York when the British Army evacuated the city in 1783 and moved to London. The proprietors sold the house in 1809 when it became the Brighton Hotel; over the years it had a variety of uses from a home for retired ministers to a boarding house. The state bought the house in the 1970s. It is managed by The Proprietary House Association.

Kennedy-Martin Farmhouse & Barn, Basking Ridge

The farmstead was built for Reverend Samuel Kennedy, a renowned local minister, in 1762. The house is one-and-a-half story wood frame, clapboard structure. Equally important to the property's historic interest is an English style barn, painted red, dating from the same period as the house. The farm was sold in 1767 to Colonel Ephraim Martin, a Revolutionary War soldier and member of New Jersey legislature. The house is now an art center owned by Bernards Township.

Wallace House, Somerville

Another of Washington's headquarters; the number of Washington headquarters in New Jersey emphasizes the important role the colony played as the crossroads of the American Revolution. More battles and skirmishes took place in New Jersey than in any other colony. The Wallace house, where Washington stayed from December 1778 to June 1779, was near the Continental Army encampment at Middlebrook, the old name for Somerville. We often hear of the Continental Army's winter suffering during the Revolutionary War, but rarely hear of the officer's partying. The *Pennsylvania Packet* newspaper wrote about social functions that "abounded in the military community scattered over the Raritan Valley that winter (after citing the names of several senior officers). They all opened their portals to the flower of the army, which met so often at the Wallace House. Many were the impromptu dances after Mrs. Washington's stately dinners. What a delight the winding Wallace staircase overlooking the wide hall was to flirting couples." The delightful house, as the newspaper called it, was built in 1778. The two-and-a-half story Dutch framed Georgian style house, covered by clapboards, was considered a palatial house for its time and location. It had eight rooms, and was owned by John Wallace, a Philadelphia fabric merchant. The home has been a house museum for more than 100 years and is now run as a state-owned historic site.

Old Dutch Parsonage, Somerville

The Old Dutch Parsonage is probably the only house in the nation where two institutions of higher learning were created and both are still going strong into their third century. They are Rutgers University and the New Brunswick Theological Seminary. The founder of the Theological Seminary, John Frelinghuysen, came to Somerville in 1751 after studying theology in the Netherlands. Besides being a minister he started a theology school in his home. The Old Dutch Parsonage, also known as the Frelinghuysen House, is considered the incubator of the New Brunswick Theology Seminary, which traces its roots to Frelinghuysen's classes held at the house from 1751 to 1754. One of his students was Jacob Hardenbergh, who became an ordained Dutch Reform Church minister and also began teaching theology classes at the house after Frelinghuysen died in 1754. He married his mentor's widow Dinah Van Bergh. His classes were held in a second floor room at the parsonage. And those classes are considered the beginning of Queens College, which later became Rutgers University. Reverend Hardenbergh was the first president of Queens College, in office from 1785 to 1790. The Georgian-style parsonage was erected for the Reverend Frelinghuysen by three Dutch Reform Churches in the Raritan Valley. The two-story brick building is laid in Flemish bond, with a cedar shake roof, and chimneys at either gable end. The house was moved several hundred yards in 1913 because it was too close to a railroad right-of-way. At the time of the move two later period frame additions were removed. An unusual feature of the house was a smokehouse in the attic, where smoke was vented through the east chimney. The house is owned by the state as an historic site.

Lime Kilns at Peapack & Stillwater

Lime Kilns, grist and other mills, along with remnants of blast furnaces and forges, are the physical reminders of our colonial manufacturing heritage, at the dawn of the Industrial Age. Lime kilns were popular in colonial and early 19th -century New Jersey in a wide swath of land that contained large amounts of limestone. Lime was used to make cement, mortar, plaster, and as a fertilizer. In the seventeenth and eighteenth centuries lime kilns were local affairs built into hillsides near where the lime would be used. The Peapack limestone kiln dates from 1794, but no doubt it is similar to mid-size kilns from the Colonial Period. It was in operation from 1794 to 1945. The smaller Stillwater kiln dates from the mid- to late- eighteenth century and is typical of kilns used to serve a small area. Lime kilns worked by loading limestone rock into the top of the kiln, while a wood fire burned in the bottom of the kiln, behind the opening archway. Lime rocks were heated to 900 degrees, releasing carbon dioxide leaving a powder of calcium oxide or quicklime sifting to the bottom of the kiln. This caustic quicklime was mixed with water into a putty-like consistency and then mixed with sand and stone to produce cement and mortar, or it could be spread on fields as a fertilizer.

Melick House, Bernards Township

The book, *Story of An Old Farm*, by a descendant of the original builder, Johannes Moelick, made the house famous. (Spelling of the last name varies from Mellick, Melick, and Moelick.) The stone house was built in 1751 by Moelick, a German farmer and tanner. He had migrated from a small town near present-day Koblenz on the Rhine River in Germany. He arrived in Philadelphia in May 1735 with his wife and four children, where the family stayed for about ten years. In 1751, Johannes bought 367 acres of land in Bedminster Township. In his book, the great, great-grandson of Johannes Moelich described the house and setting: "He erected here in the wilds of Colonial New Jersey a home like those ancient houses of masonry he had always known, bordering the banks of the winding Rhine in the far-away fatherland...it is just a quaint low house with a comely old-time presence. Almost a cottage in size—it has but nine or ten rooms— the whitewashed wall, massive enough for a citadel, are pierced in a haphazard sort of way with odd little windows...At the west end it is one-and-a-half stories high, but the slope of the hill gives another story at the eastern gable. Formerly the roof was thatched with straw. From the back porch you can see at the foot of the hill, on the east the buildings of Schomp's gristmills and sawmills. Together with their contiguous dwelling, the dam, and beautiful stream below, they present a charming rural picture." (Mellick, p. 17). Besides being an engaged farmer and tanner, Johannes Moelich was an active member and officer of Zion Lutheran Church in Tewksbury, a center of German social activity. The house was owned by the Melick family until 1893; it is privately owned.

Old House & Ranger Station, Peapack

The photochrom titled, *Old Farm, Far Hills*, was issued in 1903 by Detroit Publishing Company, an early photography publisher. The house is one-and-a-half stories, stuccoed masonry of 2,100 square feet. It was built in the mid-1700s and was a tenant house of the Schomp Farm. It is now a ranger station for Natirar Somerset County Park, a sprawling estate and grounds once owned by the King of Morocco, it was sold to Somerset County in 2003.

*Moravian Gristmill, Hope

The Moravian community of Hope began in Bethlehem, Pennsylvania, which Moravians founded in the 1740s. Missionaries from Bethlehem proselytized in New Jersey, often staying at the home of John Green in what was then called Greenland, Warren County. In 1749, Green converted and joined the Moravians who eventually bought 1,500 acres of land from him to begin their community. The first arrivals to the new community came in 1769. The placement of roads, house lots, stores, farming areas, public buildings, gristmill, and even water wells were based on a master plan. All the buildings had similar design and construction techniques; they were made of locally quarried limestone, with red brick window arches and chimneys, with steep roofs. The economic driver of the planned community was the three-story, stone gristmill, built in 1770. It was built first in order to encourage settlement and to generate income. The mill was a mini-industrial complex, with a feed, flour and fulling mills, as well as a blacksmith shop. The mill also had top-floor living quarters. The structure shows its German origins in its stonework, where only the corners and around the windows used dressed stone, the rest of the building was uncut stone. The mill was designed by Bethlehem machinist Christian Christianson. Moravians were originally from Moravia in what is now the Czech Republic, but fled to the Saxony Region of Germany to escape persecution by the Catholic rulers in 1722. Moravians trace their roots to fourteenth-century Hussite Movement, which is considered the first Protestant Church. There are mixed reports whether the Hope community was economically successful, but a small population and financial problems with the Mother Church in Germany no doubt forced the sale and abandonment of Hope in 1808; its members returned to Bethlehem.

*Moravian Church & House, Hope

Typical Moravian house, note the red brick arches above the house's windows. Hope was one of the first planned communities in North America. At its height the population reached 147. The corner stone for the church building or *Gemeinhaushe* was laid in 1781 by the Moravian Bishop from Saxony, Germany. It later became headquarters for First Hope Bank. Much of Hope retains its eighteenth century bucolic charm.

Cole's Gristmill, Pohatcong Township

The mill, in a picturesque setting alongside a tree-shaded creek, is part of the larger Hixson-Skinner Mill Complex. The mill is the only Colonial building on the site the rest of the buildings date from early-to-mid-nineteenth century. The mill was initially one-and-a-half stories, built of limestone in 1752, with walls more than two-feet thick. The two-story brick and wood addition of the 1850s is clearly visible on the mill's façade. The mill was important to the surrounding agricultural community and stayed in operation until about 1960. Basically, New Jersey had two types of gristmills, custom and merchant mills. Custom mills ground corn, wheat, and other grains for local farmers, while merchant mills ground grains into flour to sell under their own brand name or sold to other businesses. Cole's Gristmill lasted substantially longer than many water-powered, small New Jersey gristmills. Most shut down between 1870 and 1900 because they could not compete with large-scale industrial flourmills in the Midwest and also farmers shifted their crops away from grains. An historic marker in front of the mill said Pohatcong Township was first settled by Europeans in early 1700s. "They were attracted by potentially rich farmland and water power to drive mills." Pohatcong means two hills divided by a stream, in the Leni Lenape language. Not much is known about the mill's early owners. It is believed that Thomas Peterson and Robert Kennedy owned the mill jointly in the 1750s. John Hixson bought the mill in 1848. Besides the Colonial-era mill, the township also has an important number of lime kilns from the nineteenth century along the Delaware River.

Shippen Manor, Oxford

The Georgian-style manor house, on a hillside overlooking Oxford Furnace and other iron works, was built in 1755 by Dr. William Shippen Sr. and his brother Joseph Shippen Jr. The wealthy Philadelphians owned about 4,000 acres in Oxford. In 1741, the brothers joined with Jonathan Robeson, an experienced iron master, and built Oxford Furnace. The first pig iron was produced in 1743. The manor house was built a number of years after the furnace went into operation. The main section of the house is a two-and-a-half story building made of a local granite, with a slate roof and gable ends. It is 55 feet wide and 36 feet deep, with a massive stone chimney towards the rear of the main building. The two-story wing was added shortly before the Revolutionary War and is made of the same granite rock and has the same construction details as the main house, such as two-foot thick walls. Most of Shippen Manor is original. Based on its style and "construction and detailing it is clearly a product of the Delaware Valley's eighteenth century vernacular building tradition," the Nominating Petition said. The manor was a self-sufficient rural iron-working plantation surrounded by tenant farms, various mills, a store, an almost feudal lifestyle in eighteenth-century New Jersey. Joseph Shippen Jr. lived here and served as ironmaster. The manor passed through a number of hands, including the Scranton Brothers who operated the iron-making complex before founding Scranton, Pennsylvania. The site is now a house museum operated by Warren County.

Shippen Manor, Interiors

Shippen family ground floor kitchen, note all the iron implements and iron fireback; the steep, narrow stairway leading from the ground floor to first floor is known as a Jersey Twister. The first or ground floor had six rooms, while the second floor had two large bedrooms and four small bedrooms; the manor was more functional than luxurious, serving as both a home and office for the iron-making complex.

Oxford Furnace

Oxford Furnace was built about 1743 by Joseph Shippen, Dr. William Shippen, and a partner, Jonathan Robeson, a skilled ironmaster.

The furnace operated without stopping from 1743 to 1788, the longest continuous blast of any Colonial furnace. The furnace is the squat-looking building with a hipped roof, in the insert photo. It was built of rubble stone, 38 feet tall, with bosh or inside diameter of eight feet. The structure next to the furnace is known as a blowing house. The lower portion, shown in the main photo, was 30 feet high made of heavy coursed rubble stone with a graceful arch and two circular openings. The circular openings and robust construction of the building were designed to house a little known means of blowing air into furnaces, called a water blast.

No building like the blowing house exists at any other known blast furnace. The brick upper story in the insert photo housed the blast furnace's waste-heat boilers. Until the 1880s, Oxford was the major industrial and iron-mining center in Warren County. The site is owned by the state.

Zion Lutheran Church, Tewkesbury Township

Zion Lutheran Church, built in 1750, was an early and important center of German social life in what is now the Oldwick section of Tewkesbury Township, in the northern Raritan Valley. The area was originally called New Germantown (changed to Oldwick in 1918) because of the large number of German immigrants that came here from the strife-torn and highly taxed Palatine region of Germany. They came in two distinct waves, from 1714 to 1723 and again in the 1740s. At least 2,500 settled in Hunterdon and nearby Somerset counties, most were Lutherans. The Zion congregation is considered the oldest Lutheran church in the state, tracing its roots to 1714. The first church session was held at the home of Aree von Guinea, an African freedman and former slave. He gained his freedom and was living in the Raritan Valley as early as 1708. A number of notable people were members of the Zion congregation, among them Lutheran pastor Henry Melchoir Muhlenberg and Johannes Melick, the subject of the *Story of an Old Farm* book. Distinguished New York pastor Julius Falckner, the first protestant clergyman educated in America, led the congregation. The church building is a one-story fieldstone building covered with stucco, a frequently used colonial covering to protect stonework from weather. Originally, windows were small, square, and high above the ground. The current windows were put in during an 1831 church renovation. The main church entrance has a wooden gable end, with pediment, and with a wooden pilaster, that is a classical-style half column attached to a building. Frank L. Greenagel, who has written several books on New Jersey churches, estimated there are 58 churches and religious meetinghouses still standing that were built between 1703 and 1800. Zion Church is one of them and has a still active congregation.

Vought Farmstead, Clinton Township

The Johannes Vought Farmstead is the only house in the United States with intact German folk art ceilings dating from the Colonial Period. The house was built in 1759, with ornamental plaster ceilings featuring German folk art decorations, usually found on quilts, dresser drawers, and other household objects. A plaster snake in the hall is embedded into the ceiling plaster, and not added later. Four other rooms have decorative ceilings. The house with this artwork was built by Johannes Vought. It is two-and-a-half stories, made of rubble stone with a stucco surface applied in the 1830s. It has a gable end-roof. Vought came from a poverty-stricken family who immigrated from the Palatine region of Germany. Even though he was born in New Jersey, Vought's house shows German influences, such as being sited on south rising ground, with the rear of the house built into the hillside. This building style is known as a Bank House. The kitchen is in the lower level of the Bank House, with one end below grade for colder storage of food. The house was near land that could be developed as stream-irrigated meadows, also according to German-convention. Vought was an active Loyalist during the Revolutionary War. The local patriot militia arrested him in June 1776, although his son John escaped and went on to become a Captain in the Loyalist New Jersey Volunteers. Vought's property was confiscated and his farm sold in April 1779. The property changed hands several time during the eighteenth and nineteenth centuries and its original 285 acres was reduced to a 25-acre farm. An historical association is restoring the house to its original eighteenth century core, which is between the two chimneys. The house is being developed into a Loyalist Museum, the only one in New Jersey.

Vought House & Ceiling Snake

A side view of the Vought House; decorative ceiling of a plaster snake whose head faces the front door and whose body occupies the length of the hall in regularly spaced serpentine curves, with the tail at the northeast end of the hall. The house has a center hall layout, with four other rooms off the central hall having designs imbedded into their original ceilings, making this the most important Colonial house in America for German folk decorations.

Jones Tavern, Clinton Township

Thomas Jones, owner of Jones Tavern, played an important but little-known role in George Washington's successfully crossing the Delaware River and attacking Trenton on Christmas Night 1776. In a move of great foresight, as he and his weary Continental Army retreated across New Jersey towards the Delaware River and safety in Pennsylvania, Washington ordered that all boats be collected up and down the Delaware River and its tributaries. Jones and Daniel Bray gathered a number of large ore-carrying Durham boats and hid them from the British. The confiscated boats denied the British the ability to cross the Delaware River, and the Durham boats were instrumental to Washington's later successful crossing of the Delaware River. Jones was a captain in the Hunterdon County Militia and his tavern was used as a recruiting station for the patriot militia. In the early days of the Revolution the county had a substantial number of Loyalists. These Loyalists attacked Jones at his tavern beat him, threatened his family, and stole money on the night of June 24, 1776. The Loyalists were led by John Vought (see page 62). The tavern was converted from Jones' farmhouse in 1767, and was located on a busy road connecting Easton, Pennsylvania to New Brunswick. The original house is the two-story stone section, with gable roof. The two- story wood-frame section was added at an unknown date and a third story of wood frame and shingle construction was added to it later in the nineteenth century. The former tavern is a small office building today.

Old Stone Mill, Franklin Township

The mill and the entire hamlet of Pittstown were owned by Moore Furman since 1764. Furman was Deputy Quartermaster General of Provisions for New Jersey, from 1778 to 1780, helping to coordinate the Continental army's supply network during the Revolutionary War. Furman made Pittstown (part of Franklin Township) a major supply depot and milling center for the Continental Army. Furman was born in Hopewell Township, in 1728, but moved to Trenton as a young man. By 1757 he was the town's postmaster and also high sheriff. Furman has been called Trenton's most distinguished eighteenth century businessman. He was Trenton's first mayor in 1792. Furman named Pittstown after William Pitt, Earl of Chatham, a British supporter in Parliament of the American cause. Pittstown was previously known as Hoff's Mill, founded in the 1740s as a milling center, with a tavern and shop, all owned by Charles Hoff Jr. In debt, Hoff sold all his businesses to Moore Furman in 1764. Furman owned the town until his death in 1808. His gristmill was built in 1778 to provide flour for Washington's encampments throughout New Jersey. The stone portion is the original mill, which is made of rough-cut stone, two-and-a-half stories high, with a broad gable facing towards a lane that ran off the main Pittstown Road. The water wheel was located beneath the mill; the hoist hood extends from the front gable. The mill was owned by several different families and apparently operated until 1928. The mill building is still in use as a swimming pool supply business.

Office Building, Union Iron Works, High Bridge

Union Iron Works was an important New Jersey blast furnace and forge that evolved from a single blast furnace in 1742 to the large Taylor-Wharton Iron and Steel Company complex that was in business until 1972. The company was founded on December 1, 1741, when wealthy Philadelphians William Allen and Joseph Turner bought 10,000 acres of land from the West Jersey Proprietors to set up a blast furnace. Earlier, Allen had been mayor of Philadelphia from 1735–1736. The office building was erected in 1743 and also served as a company store and infirmary. The building was the administrative center of the two iron furnaces, two forges, and iron mining business of Union Iron Works. The original building was a two-and-a-half story stone structure, with gable ends. In the 1890s a wing was added to the right side of the building. In the 1920s a third story was added and the roofline was changed to a hipped roof. In the 1930s a porch was removed and new entrance archway installed. During the Revolutionary War the owners of Union Iron Works were strong Loyalists. However, Union Iron Works superintendent, Robert Taylor, was a supporter of the rebellion and supplied the Continental Army with cannon balls. The Iron Works and its property were seized in 1778 by the New Jersey government because of Allen and Turner's Loyalist activities. Superintendent Taylor was selected as one of the commissioners to sell the confiscated property. He bought one of the forges and 360 acres of land that became the basis for the Taylor Iron and Steel Co. (TISCO). The company lasted until 1972 under the Taylor family, as the Taylor- Wharton Iron and Steel Company. The office building, owned by the township, has been sitting idle since 1972.

Ironmaster's House & Solitude House, High Bridge

Top, ironmaster's House at Union Iron Works, built about 1740 of stone covered by stucco. Below is the stone, two-story Solitude House, built about 1745 as a residence for the owners of Union Iron Works. During the Revolutionary War the building served as a house-arrest site for Royal Governor John Penn of Pennsylvania and New Jersey's Chief Colonial Justice, Benjamin Chew.

Eversole-Hall House, Readington Township

The Charles Eversole house is important because it is average. It represents the way a middle class family lived in the eighteenth century. The farmhouse shows the merging of architectural traditions of Hunterdon County's various ethnic groups from England, Holland, Germany, and France. The mixing of architectural styles began in the 1750s, and is reflected in this house built in 1770. The one-and-a-half story, wooden frame, clapboard house is one room deep, with an enclosed rear porch and open front porch. It has two interior end brick chimneys. The Nominating Petition said: "The rectangular frame, stone, or brick house of one-and-a-half to two stories, with two of three rooms on each floor, a side gable, and interior end chimneys became more or less standard" for this part of Hunterdon County. Charles Eversole, the original owner of the house, was born in 1731 in Berg, France and emigrated to Philadelphia by 1753. Eversole moved to Readington in 1768. He was a member of the Zion Lutheran Church in Oldwick. Eversole died in 1805 and his house was sold to pay off debts. Over the years, several Eversole relatives owned the house until it was sold in April 1832 to Abraham Hall. A number of people owned the farm after Hall, until the township bought the property in 1988.

Rockingham, Franklin Township, Somerset County

Rockingham was George Washington's final headquarters in New Jersey. He lived here from July to November 1783, when nearby Princeton was the capital of the United States. He wrote his famous farewell address to the Army here in November 1783. His final sentence in the address was: "with these wishes, and this benediction, the Commander in Chief is about to retire from service. The curtain of separation will soon be drawn—and the military scene to him will be closed forever." The house George and Martha Washington lived in was a vernacular, two-story, wooden-framed, clapboard covered building. It had a center chimney, a wooden shingle roof with gable ends. Its two-story balcony piazza dominates the house. There is controversy about when the house was built, some sources said 1710, others said 1734; regardless, it is one the oldest homes in the Millstone River Valley. It was originally built by Jedediah Higgins family and was added onto by a subsequent owner, John Berrian, an Associate Justice of the New Jersey Supreme Court. He lived here from 1734 to his death in 1761. His widow stayed in the house and rented it to the Continental Congress who in turn had George and Martha Washington live there. The house has been moved three times, threatened by adjacent quarrying operations. After several owners, the Washington Headquarters Association bought it in 1897. Rockingham is now owned by the state as an historical site.

Nassau Hall, Princeton

Nassau Hall was built between 1754–1756, and when it was finished the entire Princeton University community could fit inside: classrooms, administrative offices, dormitories, and a dining section. Princeton University was founded in Elizabeth in 1743 as the College of New Jersey (no relation to the state college that usurped the name today). It was in Newark for a period before moving to Princeton in 1756. Its first building was the largest and most impressive building in the Middle Colonies. Nassau Hall served as a model for many other university buildings around the country. It was also the scene of fighting during the Battle of Princeton on January 3, 1777. Nassau Hall was the capitol of the United States when the Continental Congress met here from July to November 1783. The building was designed by Dr. William Shippen (see page 58) and Robert Smith of Philadelphia, whose work included Carpenter's Hall in Philadelphia. Smith is credited with most of the design and supervised construction. William Worth, a local mason, did the stonework on the rectangular hall that was 177 feet in width and approximately 55 feet deep. The Hall is named after British King William III of the House of Nassau. The building was twice gutted by fires that only left exterior walls standing. After a fire in 1802, well-known architect Henry Latrobe restored the building. Latrobe was the first professionally trained American architect and a proponent of the Federal style. After the 1856 fire, John Notman, restored the building but made substantial changes, including adding a cupola on the roof. The Nominating Petition said: "the stone walls which endured the Battle of Princeton and two fires, retain the basic strength and simplicity that characterized their original appearance." Today, the National Historic Landmark is used for Princeton University administrative offices.

President's House, Princeton

MacLean House, also called President's House, on Princeton University campus was designed by Robert Smith who built Nassau Hall. The two-story, Georgian-style brick building with gable ends was built in 1756. The building has retained its original appearance except for a porch added in 1868. It was home to John Witherspoon president of the university from 1768 to 1779, and signer of the Declaration of Independence. The National Historic Landmark houses Princeton University's alumni association. It is being renovated.

Bainbridge House, Princeton

Job Stockton, a tanner and cousin to Richard Stockton who was a signer of the Declaration of Independence, built this attractive Georgian house in 1766. The two-story, wood-frame house has a brick façade, with the other three sides red-painted clapboard. The gable roof has two internal chimneys at either end. The house remains unaltered except for a small rear addition. Inside, a mantel, floorboards and fireplace are all original. By 1774, Job's cousin Richard Stockton had inherited the house. He rented the house to Dr. Absalon Bainbridge a physician and a Loyalist. Shortly after renting the house, a son William was born to Absalom on May 17, 1774. William eventually became a Naval Commodore, commanding the USS *Constitution*, "Old Ironsides," in the War of 1812. He gained fame for his battles against the Barbary pirates off the coast of North Africa. The house is named after him. Because of his increasingly unpopular Loyalist activities, Dr. Absalon Bainbridge fled to New York City. His brother, Dr. Ebenezer Bainbridge, took over the lease. When the British occupied Princeton in December 1776 General William Howe made his headquarters at the house. Members of the Continental Congress lived here in July through November 1783 when Princeton was the capital of the new United States. The house is now headquarters for the Princeton Historical Society.

Morven, Princeton

Morven is one of the most famous houses in New Jersey, official governor's residence, one of the early Georgian mansions, and home to the prominent Stockton family. Richard Stockton, signer of the Declaration of Independence, was born here in 1730 and called Morven home until his death in 1781. He was a successful attorney and state Supreme Court Justice. He was married to Annis Boudinot, whose brother Elias was president of the Continental Congress. The original house was built in stages by his father between 1701 and 1709, with Richard making further changes until 1775. The original center section of the house reached its present look in 1775. The two-story, original section is 46 feet wide and 34 feet deep. Two brick flanking wings were added, one in the late 1700s the other in 1848, the Greek Revival style front porch was also added in 1848. The outside porch door leads into a center hall that extends the depth of the house and joins with a rear-stair hall that runs along the width of the house thus linking both wings to the main house. The interior largely dates from the late eighteenth or early nineteenth centuries and has been repaired twice after fires during the Revolutionary War and again in 1821. The Stockton family owned the house until 1945 when New Jersey Governor Walter Edge bought it. He donated Morven to the state in 1954 to be used as a governor's mansion, which function it served until 1981, when Drumthwacket, also located in Princeton, became the official Governor's Mansion. Morven, a National Historic Landmark, is now a house museum.

Thomas Clarke House, Princeton

The Clarke farmhouse was in the midst of the Battle of Princeton, January 3, 1777. The battle developed in the early morning when Washington's troops, who had outfoxed the British in the Second Battle of Trenton and escaped certain defeat by leaving campfires burning and sneaking away on back roads from their positions in Trenton to Princeton. British units led by Colonel Charles Mawhood patrolling Clarke's farm surprised the Americans. The initial British assault drove the Continentals into retreat until Washington appeared, and riding between the opposing forces rallied his men. As more American soldiers arrived on the scene, they counter-attacked driving the British back into Princeton. The fighting engulfed the town, with some of it taking place on the university campus and even inside Nassau Hall. The British were forced out of Princeton and retreated to New Brunswick, while Washington's weary troops marched to Morristown and winter quarters. The house where the battle began was built about 1770 by Thomas Clarke, a Quaker farmer, who lived on the 200-acre farm with his sisters Sarah and Hannah. The two-story, frame house covered by clapboards, with a gable roof, is described as "half Georgian." It served as a field hospital during the Battle of Princeton. American Brigadier General Hugh Mercer died in a second floor bedroom on January 12, 1777, from wounds he received in the battle. Mercer County is named after him. The National Historic Landmark Clarke house opened to the public in 1976 as a state historic site.

Presbyterian Church of Lawrenceville

The two-story, white-painted brick Presbyterian Church was built in 1764. The rectangular church was originally 45 feet wide and 32 feet deep, with a slate, gable ended-roof, topped by a cupola. Following an 1833 expansion, the depth was increased to 75 feet. The church history said many notables attended services here, and on December 31, 1713, John Hart, a signer of the Declaration of Independence, was baptized here. The church was precursor of the nearby Lawrenceville Prep School when in 1810 its minister, Isaac Brown, started the Maidenhead Academy to prepare young men for college. This academy developed into the Lawrenceville Preparatory School. The church cemetery has several Revolutionary War dead buried there. The church congregation was organized in 1698, with the first church built on this site in 1709 in a meetinghouse style. The first church also served as a county courthouse for a period. Shown on the right is the main entrance to the church.

Johnson Ferry House, Washington Crossing State Park

Johnson Ferry House is another building associated with George Washington. It was here the Continental Army landed after crossing the stormy, ice-choked Delaware River on Christmas night 1776 to attack the Hessians in Trenton. Washington undoubtedly took refuge in the house and waited nervously as the crossing took hours more than anticipated. Understanding eighteenth century ferry crossings can be confusing. The ferry or crossing site is named for its departure point, thus Washington's troops crossed the Delaware River from McConkey's ferry in Pennsylvania arriving at Johnson Ferry House in New Jersey. Older references call the house McConkey's Ferry House when it should be called Johnson Ferry House. Rutger Jansen, of Dutch descent from Flatbush, New York, built the house in 1740. It is a one-and-a-half story frame house, sheathed in scallop shingles, with a gambrel roof, and a large central brick chimney. The exterior is considered a good example of a vernacular Dutch farmhouse. The interior was extensively remodeled in the 1930s as a WPA project. The house was set among a 480-acre farm that bordered the Delaware River. The Dutch name Jensen was Americanized to Johnson. Rutger's son Garret inherited the farm in 1748 and created the ferry business and tavern. At his death in 1766, financial problems forced his sons to sell the farm and businesses. In 1770, Abraham Harvey bought the property and then rented it to James Slack who lived here when Washington made his famous Christmas night 1776 crossing of the Delaware River. Abraham Harvey reclaimed operation of the farm and ferry in 1786 and operated it until 1801. After changing hands several times, the state bought the house in 1919 and incorporated it into Washington Crossing State Park, which is a National Historic Landmark.

Old Barracks, Trenton

The army barracks at Trenton was one of five barracks built during the French and Indian War to house British soldiers. Other barracks were built between 1758–1759 at Burlington, New Brunswick, Perth Amboy, and Elizabeth. The barracks were erected after vociferous citizen complaints about being forced to house British soldiers, sometimes as many as 10 to a house, during the French and Indian War, which lasted from 1754 to 1763. Whether New Jersey Colony or British government would pay for the barracks was an ongoing friction between the General Assembly and Royal authorities. The Trenton Barracks was designed to provide quarters for 300 soldiers, their officers and equipment. It is a large two-and-half story, U-shaped building, made mostly of fieldstone, but with a brick two-and-a-half story Georgian-style house attached as an officer's billet. A narrow, two-level balcony extends around the inner side of the barracks. The longer sides are 136 feet long and 20 feet wide. During the Revolutionary War, depending on who controlled Trenton, the Barracks were occupied by American, British, and Hessian soldiers. The Battle of Trenton, December 26, 1776, swirled around the barracks. The barracks was later used for sick and wounded American soldiers, some 600 were brought here after the siege of Yorktown, Virginia, in November 1781. The colonial barracks were sold at auction in 1786. Trenton Barracks was subdivided into apartments until it was bought and restored piecemeal by a preservation group and the state between 1899 and its opening to the public in 1917. The Barracks is a National Historic Landmark.

William Trent House, Trenton

Trent House, home of the founder of Trenton, is one of the earliest Georgian-style houses in New Jersey, built in 1719. The two-story brick mansion has Flemish bond on the front—the other sides are in English bond brickwork. The 40 feet by 48 feet house has a low-pitched hipped roof, with a six-sided cupola on top. Inside there are four rooms on each floor. Despite his prominence, not much is known of William Trent's early life except that he was born in Scotland in 1666 or thereabouts, and was living in Philadelphia by 1693. He was a speculator, ship owner, merchant, and slave trader, who became wealthy and dabbled in both New Jersey and Pennsylvania politics. William Trent built the house as a summer home at the Falls of the Delaware River. He moved into the house fulltime in 1721 and that is considered the founding of Trenton. Two years later, he became New Jersey's first resident Chief Justice. Trent died on Christmas day 1724 from "a fit of apoplexy." After Trent's death a number of prominent families occupied the mansion, including New Jersey's first Royal Governor, Lewis Morris (before that as a Royal Colony New York's governor was also New Jersey's) from 1742 to 1746, when the mansion was called Bloomsbury Court. During the Revolutionary War the house changed hands several times, depending on who controlled Trenton. In the 1800s, two New Jersey governors lived here, Philemon Dickinson (1835–1838) and Rodman McCamley (1854 to 1857) when the house was called Woodlawn. The last private owner, Edward A. Stokes, donated the house to the city in 1929 with the proviso the house be returned to its 1719 look. The National Historic Landmark is now a city-run house museum.

Trent House Interiors

The Trent House grand entry staircase leading to the second floor shows a simple elegance. The kitchen has an eighteenth-century automated rotisserie inside the fireplace. The rotisserie operated by a rope pulley, with winding device on the mantle, to create rotation without cooks constantly cranking the rotisserie; also note the beehive oven inside the far wall.

Francis Hopkinson House, Bordentown

An historic marker in front of the Francis Hopkinson house almost breathlessly recited his accomplishments: "...famous Revolutionary War patriot, a signer of the Declaration of Independence, originator of the Great Seal of the State of New Jersey, member of Congress, statesman, artist, musician and satirist." In that latter role, Hopkinson wrote the famous Revolutionary War ditty, "The Battle of the Kegs," satirizing British naval operations on the Delaware River. Hopkinson was born on October 2, 1737, in Philadelphia, son of a prominent lawyer. He was graduated with the first class at College of Philadelphia in 1757, which later became the University of Pennsylvania. He was an attorney and in 1776 he was elected to the Continental Congress and for two years there he was chairman of the Naval Board. He held other posts during the Revolution. He was also well known as a musician and published poet, as well as an accomplished artist who designed or aided in designing the Great Seal of the United States, the New Jersey State Seal, the U.S. Treasury Department Seal, and others. Hopkinson lived in his father-in-law's house from 1774 to 1791. Hopkinson had married Ann Borden, daughter of the richest man in Bordentown, where he practiced law. The house he lived in was built in 1750 and was originally owned by John Imlay, a merchant. It is an L-shaped two- and- a half story brick building, with a gambrel roof and dormers. The main house is 41 feet wide and 30 feet deep, a two-story wing, also made of brick, extends to the rear. The interior arrangement is center hall, but it has been substantially altered as an office building, although the exterior of the house is little changed. The house is a National Historic Landmark.

Cooper & Lawrence Houses, Burlington

Two adjacent row houses in Burlington City had famous sons born in them. In slightly different time periods writer James Fenimore Cooper and Naval hero James Lawrence were born there.

Even if it were not for the notable births, the townhouses would be important because both are significant examples of early American urban living spaces. The two townhouses share a common wall and both are two- and- a -half story brick buildings, covered with painted stucco. They are a mixture of Federal and Georgian styles, common in South Jersey urban houses.The Lawrence House was built sometime between 1742 and 1769, while the Cooper House (see drawing) was built about 1780.

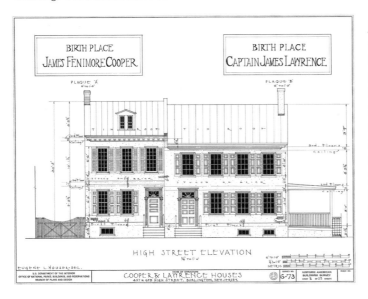

James Fenimore Cooper, considered America's first novelist, was born here on September 15, 1789. Next door, James Lawrence, naval hero in the War of 1812 was born here on October 1, 1781. Cooper and Lawrence Houses are now owned by the Burlington County Historical Society.

Revell House, Burlington City

One of the few seventeenth century houses remaining in New Jersey, the Revell House was built in 1685. The one-and-a-half story brick building is considered the oldest house in Burlington County. It is 26 feet wide by 16 feet, deep, with a gambrel roof and two shed dormers. Originally, the house had a gable roof, the gambrel roof was added sometime in the eighteenth century. Inside there is one room on the first floor with two corner fireplaces, a Jersey Winder staircase leads to the second floor, which has two rooms. The house was built for George Hutchinson, an influential and wealthy West Jersey proprietor, and later sold to Thomas Revel. It is believed Revell never lived in the house during his ownership from 1696 to 1699, but used it as an office. He held a number of posts after Burlington City became the capital of West Jersey Province in 1681. Revell was the first clerk of the West Jersey Assembly, the first Burlington County Recorder, and Registrar for the West Jersey Proprietors. In 1703, when West Jersey became a crown colony he was appointed to the Governor's Council. Revell sold the house in 1699 to Isaac De Cou, Surveyor General of New Jersey, who lived in it for many years. He was responsible for the symmetrical plan for Burlington City, with a main street, now High Street, that ran at a right angle to the Delaware River, with ten lots on either side of the street. The lots on the eastside of the street were for Yorkshire Quaker settlers and those on the westside for London Quakers. Revell House was moved to its present site in 1966. The house is owned by a local chapter of the Daughters of the American Revolution.

Three Tuns Tavern, Mount Holly

One of the few taverns in New Jersey that has been in business since Colonial days. The tavern was built in 1723. It is a two-and-a-half story, rectangular brick building set in Flemish bond, with a gable roof and three dormers. The tavern was probably built by Samuel Briant, the first owner, who sold the tavern in 1737 to Josiah White. The tavern was the starting point for stagecoaches traveling over the Monmouth Road to shore points. Based on its original name, the stagecoach stop must have been a boon to business, for tun is an old English word or measure of a barrel of beer or ale. A Tun is approximately 250 gallons, so a three-tun tavern probably meant it sold a lot of beer and ale and was a popular spot. The tavern had its critics, including John Woolman, one of Mount Holly's most famous citizens, a prominent Quaker preacher, writer, and strong abolitionist. Woolman wrote in his journal that he "remonstrated with the landlord of the (Three Tun) tavern for the noise, disorder, and evil actions."(Bastien, p. 57). There is no record of the results of Woolman's complaints. When Mount Holly was occupied during the Revolutionary War the tavern was Hessian headquarters. In the last year or so of the American Revolution the tavern was used for the British Court of Admiralty. The tavern has operated under various names over the years, and was closed for a period during Prohibition; its current name is Mill Street Hotel and Tavern.

Ridgway House & Fire Station, Mount Holly

Both Mount Holly buildings are under appreciated. John Ridgway House, built in 1760 for the Surveyor General of West Jersey, is important as a rare middle class, freestanding-townhouse. The old fire department building, a shed-like 8 by 12 feet, housed an early fire engine for the Relief Fire Company, the oldest active volunteer fire department in the nation, founded in 1752, the same date the firehouse was built; it is on the grounds of Relief Fire Co.

Old Schoolhouse, Mount Holly

Brainerd School is the oldest schoolhouse in New Jersey, built in 1759. The vernacular Georgian-style building is also known as the Old Schoolhouse. It is a one-story, patterned brick structure, laid in Flemish bond. It has a gable roof. The schoolhouse is 24 feet wide by 20 feet deep containing a single classroom with a fireplace against the rear wall. The one-room school is typical for Colonial and early American elementary school buildings. New Jersey had no colony-wide educational laws, but left the schooling of its youngsters up to each town, unlike Massachusetts that had laws requiring education of children, dating back to 1647. Towns did make an effort to educate their children and there are a number of examples of local education laws, such as Elizabethtown in 1669, "100 acres of land be set aside for education." Even these town-encouraged primary schools were often sectarian and funded by private subscription. The Mount Holly school, founded June 26, 1759, by five trustees was funded by subscription of one pound per week per child. It was open to all and drew children from varied backgrounds. John Woolman, who taught at the school in the 1760s, is probably Mount Holly's most famous resident. He lived here from 1720 to 1772 and was an ardent abolitionist and is considered one of the most-revered Quaker ministers of the Colonial era. His journal is full of acute observations, philosophical musings, and is considered important enough to be included in the Harvard Classics, as the *Journal of John Woolman*. The school was run by various private groups until 1913 when it became a public school. It was donated to the Colonial Dames of America in 1951.

Kirby Mill, Medford

Kirby Mill, also known as Haines Mill, was built in 1778 by John Haines. The complex grew to also include a sawmill, blacksmith and wheelwright shops, and a cider mill. The four-story, wood-frame mill was originally 40 feet deep and 66 feet wide; it was built using massive beams and wooden pegs. Under various owners, the mill was in operation until 1968 grinding feed for local farmers. The Medford Historical Society owns it.

Arneytown Tavern, North Hanover Township

Arneytown Tavern entered the public record in 1752 when William Lawrie deeded it to his son-in-law, Richard Platt. It was obviously built before then and was most likely Lawrie's house. Most taverns in New Jersey were converted from private houses. The main section of the tavern is wood frame, two-and-half story clapboard building, measuring 50 feet wide by 32 feet deep. It is a center hall design with two rooms on each side of the hall. A wing to the right side of the main house is one-and-a-half stories, and is 40 feet wide and 34 feet deep. The addition has been used as a post office, grocery store, and feed store. Both sections have gable roofs; the main section has two inside end chimneys. Inside chimneys, that is chimneys rising to the roofline inside the house, were common as an effort to use chimney heat to warm the house. The tavern was a stop on the stagecoach line running from Trenton to the shore. It was also used by the sheriffs of Burlington and Monmouth counties for auctions of delinquent properties and forfeited goods because of its convenient location on Provincetown Road that divided the counties and was also the division line between West Jersey and East Jersey. Arneytown, originally called Upper Freehold Township, developed along Provincetown Road by its early Quaker settlers. It is a rural hamlet still and has little modern development, thus a number of its eighteenth century homes are well preserved. Arneytown tavern stood idle for a number of years but has recently been renovated and is now a private home. There is some issue how the town got its name, Arney was either an early settler's first or last name.

Craig House, Freehold

The Revolutionary War Battle of Monmouth, part of which took place on Samuel and John Craig's farm on a hot June 28, 1778, spawned one of the endearing stories of the American Revolution, that of Molly Pitcher. Heroine Molly is generally depicted bringing water to American troops or swabbing a field cannon in midst of the action. The battle Molly and her Continental soldiers fought began when Lt. General Henry Clinton commanding 17,000 British troops and miles of supply wagons evacuated Philadelphia. The British column was making its way across Burlington and Monmouth counties to linkup with ships waiting for them in Sandy Hook Bay. General Washington and 13,000 Continentals left Valley Forge in pursuit, meeting the British in central Monmouth County. General Charles Lee and his advance units of 5,000 soldiers clashed with the British Army rearguard and were forced into a disorganized rout, until Washington arrived on the scene, rallied the soldiers and counter-attacked. Historians consider the Battle a draw, as the British continued to Sandy Hook, but it proved American soldiers could stand up to British regulars. Lee was court martialed for his failure of leadership at Monmouth and his army career ended. The Craig house was used as a field hospital by British forces, even though John fought with the Americans. The home turned hospital was built in two stages, first between 1704 and 1717 of one-and-a-half stories, covered with clapboards. The larger section was added in 1747 and was also wood-framed, two-and-a-half stories, with shingles on the front. Besides its role in the Battle of Monmouth, the Craig house is important because it represents a typical New Jersey English-style farmhouse. It is on the grounds of Monmouth Battlefield State Park, which is a National Historic Landmark.

Tennent Church, Manalapan

The First Presbyterian Church, also known as Old Tennent Church, was in the midst of the Battle of Monmouth on June 28, 1778 (see page 88). The church was located on high ground, northwest of the American positions and was in the line of retreat of General Lee. It was used as a hospital for Continental Army soldiers. The church is remarkably well preserved and stands as a silent witness to the great battle that took place beneath its spire. The oak-frame church, sheathed in long cedar shingles, with a steep slate roof topped by a small tower, is considered to be one story with gallery. It was 60 feet long by 40 feet wide, and seated 400 people. It was built between 1751 to 1753 by master carpenter John Davies. The church is named after ministers John Tennent and his brother William Tennent. John was minister from 1730 to 1732, and William was the preacher from 1733 to 1777. The church was chartered on January 21, 1749, by King George II. At that time, the church adopted a seal with the phrase "Religious Liberty." It still functions as a Presbyterian Church.

Village Inn, Englishtown

The Village Inn, also called Davis Tavern, is a much-altered building that at its core was built in 1732 as two-and-half story frame building, clapboard covered. Its initial owner was Robert Newell, who was a tailor and member of Tennent's Presbyterian Church. In 1749 Newell sold the house to Thomas Davies whose son was the chief architect of Tennent's Presbyterian Church. Thomas had pew number one at the church indicating his importance to the community. Thomas Davis willed the property to his son, Moses Davies, who by 1766 had converted the house into a tavern. The tavern had two additions in 1815, and was remodeled in a Federal-style. In 1934, the tavern was again remodeled bringing it back into a Colonial style or at least to what people in the 1930s thought was a Colonial style. The Nominating Petition said of the house: "The village Inn is a building which has evolved since the eighteenth century. Its character is cumulative in the sense that owners have added to and subtracted from the building over the years to accommodate changing building use, style, and changing attitudes toward the use of space. At the core of the building is as an eighteenth-century two-room Dutch framed vernacular house." The tavern is important today as a building that was part of the Battle of Monmouth, and as a reminder not to tinker too much with buildings that have an important link to our collective past. The tavern looks today the way we in the twenty-first century (just like the 1930s) think a colonial tavern should look. There are a number of fictions on the internet about the tavern's role in the aftermath of General Lee's cowardice at the Battle of Monmouth. The Battleground Historical Society acquired the building in 1978.

Old Yellow Baptist Meetinghouse, Upper Freehold Township

The distinctive Yellow Meetinghouse, set at the edge of a cemetery, with a green parsonage house farther back presents a pastoral scene that is little changed today from the mid-1700s. The Baptist Meetinghouse, now called Old Yellow Meetinghouse, was built in 1750s replacing an earlier meetinghouse that was built in approximately 1720. The cemetery in the foreground has graves of soldiers dating from the French and Indian War until World War II. The Yellow Meetinghouse was built on precise compass points, with the two gable ends facing east and west, thus giving a longer southern exposure for both light and heat. The vernacular, rectangular building is 46 feet wide by 26 feet deep and 32 feet high. It is wood-frame construction covered by clapboards, painted yellow. The Baptists who settled here were yeoman farmers who moved inland from their coastal settlement at Middletown, one of the initial six New Jersey towns settled after the Dutch defeat in 1664. The other towns were Raritan, also settled by Baptists, Shrewsbury, settled by Quakers, and Newark, Elizabethtown, and Wood Bridge, all settled by Puritans of English descent. The Baptists who moved inland were members of the Middletown Baptist Congregation. The green parsonage, now empty, was home of the minister of the Old Yellow Meetinghouse. It is a two-story framed building with cedar shingles, there are two fireplaces at the gable ends; the house was built in the late eighteenth century. The Meetinghouse was restored in 1992 and is only used a couple times a year for special occasions.

Allen House, Shrewsbury

The Allen house occupies one corner of an historic intersection in Shrewsbury, Broad Street and Sycamore Avenue. Besides the Allen house, the intersection has two Colonial era houses of worship, a Quaker Meetinghouse and the Wren-inspired Christ Episcopal Church. Shrewsbury, initially settled by Quakers, was one of the original six New Jersey towns. The house is a rare seventeenth-century residence built between 1670 and 1688 by Judah Allen. It is a wood-frame, two-and- a -half stories, coved by shingles, with a gambrel roof.

The house has had additions over the years. In 1754, after several different owners, Josiah Halstead bought the house and converted it into a tavern, known as Sign of the Blue Ball. In 1779, a dozen patriot soldiers were based in the tavern as a town guard when Loyalists from Sandy Hook launched a surprise attack in the middle of the night killing three soldiers and taking nine as prisoners. The house has been restored to its 1750s look. The photo is of the rear of the house, while the drawing shows the front.

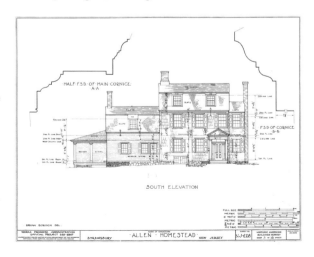

Christ Episcopal Church, Shrewsbury

The attractive Christopher Wren-inspired church with tower and steeple was designed by well-known Philadelphia builder and architect, Robert Smith who designed Carpenter's Hall in Philadelphia. He also designed and supervised construction of President's House (see page 71) and Nassau Hall, (see page 70) both at Princeton University. The Georgian-style church was built in 1769 of wooden frame, covered by cedar shingles. The main body is 62 feet by 32 feet, with sidewalls rising two stories. The rooftop octagon cupola is the same as the cupola at Carpenter's Hall. The church has had a couple of expansions, and as the Nominating Petition said "in spite of periodic alterations, a very substantial amount of eighteenth century fabric remains, primarily because work crews have reused and recycled earlier materials during subsequent renovations." The congregation traces its roots to Lewis Morris, later governor of New Jersey. Morris complained to the Anglican Bishop of London that Quakers had their own meetinghouse and Anglicans here needed a church also. He was listened to. At the start of the Revolutionary War the minister, Reverend Samuel Cooke, was a Loyalist. He was forced to flee to New York City where he became a chaplain in the British Army. The church was used as a barracks for American soldiers during the war. It is a still active Episcopal Church.

Sandy Hook Lighthouse, Gateway National Recreation Area

Sandy Hook is the oldest operating lighthouse in the nation, first lighted on June 11, 1764. It marked the entrance to outer New York Harbor, a role it still performs. The 103- foot lighthouse is built of whitewashed rubble stone in an octagon shape with a base diameter of 29 feet gradually tapering to 15 feet diameter at top. The light is housed in a red lantern on top of the tower. The keeper's quarters are adjacent to the lighthouse, and was erected in 1883, replacing an earlier building. Sandy Hook Lighthouse was originally called New York Lighthouse because New York City businessmen and ship owners sponsored it. It was paid for by a series of New York City lotteries and maintained by a levy of three-pence per ton for ships entering the harbor. The builder was master mason, Isaac Conro, and at the time of construction it was the nation's fifth lighthouse. During the Revolutionary War the British held the lighthouse most of the time. In June 1776, Americans fired artillery at the lighthouse hoping to damage it and render it useless to the British. The artillery officer later reported he "found the walls so firm that the canon [sic] fire could make no impression." The exterior of the lighthouse looks exactly as it did the day it went into service, but winds, shifting sands and the sea have elongated the barrier island and now the lighthouse is more than one-and-a-half miles from the shoreline; it was built only 500 feet from New York Harbor's shoreline. In 1789 the new U.S. government took over operation of all lighthouses, marking the beginning of the U.S. Lighthouse Service, which lasted until 1939 when it was merged with the Coast Guard. The lighthouse is a National Historic Landmark.

Cavalry Cottage, Stafford Township

The vernacular one-and-a-half story, wood-frame house was built in 1760. It is one of the oldest houses in Ocean County. The original rectangular building had two rooms on the ground floor, with a sleeping loft above them. The house is a combination of Dutch and English building techniques, with Dutch framing and the rest English-style construction. The core house has had two additions, one in the early nineteenth century, when a one story kitchen and small pantry were added to the back in a lean-to fashion. In 1882, a front porch was added along with a shed dormer on the roof. The black and white photo, taken in 1945, shows both the porch and dormer additions. These additions were later removed. Brigadier General William N. Greer lived in the house from 1872 to 1873. Grier came here in 1872 to be near his daughter and son-in law. He was graduated from West Point in 1835 and served as a cavalry officer in the Mexican War and Civil War. The house changed hands a number of times, including use as a summer cottage, until Stafford Township bought the house in 2003.

Pomona Hall, Camden

The attractive Georgian-style brick house was built by Joseph Cooper Jr., the grandson of William Cooper, founder of Camden. The house was built in two phases, initially by the grandson in 1726, of two-and-a-half stories brick, laid in Flemish bond.

The house had a steep pitched roof with dormers. Inside, there were two rooms on each floor. Joseph was active in county politics and served in the General Assembly from 1730 to 1749. In 1788, Joseph's cousin, Marmaduke Cooper, inherited the house and added a central hall and two rooms. The house is approximately 58 feet wide and 37 feet deep. Marmaduke was active in the patriot cause, until the Philadelphia Meeting of Quakers advised all Quakers not to participate in the Revolution and to be conscientious objectors.

His house is considered an important example of eighteenth century New Jersey architecture. The city-owned building is leased to the Camden County Historical Society, which operates it as a house museum.

Indian King Tavern, Haddonfield

The Indian King Tavern is proclaimed as the site where New Jersey became a state. On September 20, 1777, the Colonial General Assembly meeting at the tavern, "resolved, thereafter the word state should be substituted for colony in all public writs and commissions." Some historians have argued New Jersey's 1776 constitution made it a state and the action at the tavern was simply legal housekeeping. Earlier that year, in May 1777 the provincial General Assembly meeting at the tavern adopted the state's official seal (see page 15), which is still in use today with some minor alterations. The tavern was host to an assortment of governmental and political meetings because its second floor hall was the largest non-religious space in the colony. The tavern was built in 1750 by Matthias Aspden, a Philadelphia merchant and shop owner, and also a Loyalist. In the early days of the Revolution, Aspden sold the tavern to Thomas Redman. At that time, the tavern consisted of two connected buildings; a three-story section was built in 1750. The two-and-a-half story section was built in 1764, and is four bays wide. A bay is an architectural measure describing a façade. A bay is either a window or a door so three bays could be two windows and a door. Both buildings are yellow paint over stucco. The original house was three stories with two rooms on each floor; a kitchen and cellar were also part of the original tavern. It was named Indian King after a defunct Haddonfield tavern that used the name to honor Lenni Lenape Indian chiefs who once lived in the area. The tavern officially became the state's first historic site in June 1903.

Whitall House, Red Bank Battlefield

The farm of wealthy Quakers Anne and James Whitall was the site of the little-known Revolutionary War battle of Red Bank. In April 1777, the farm was taken over by the Pennsylvania Militia who built Fort Mercer there. The earthen fortification was built under the direction of Polish military engineer General Thaddeus Kosciuszko. Across the river, opposite the Whitall farmhouse, Fort Mifflin was already functioning. The row galleys of the Pennsylvania Navy as well as several forts had controlled the lower Delaware River and blocked any advance of British ships planning to attack Philadelphia. The British outflanked the Delaware defenses, however, and in late September 1777 sailed to the head of navigation of Chesapeake Bay at Elkton, Maryland, marched overland and seized Philadelphia. In order to bring vital supplies to Philadelphia the British began a series of attacks to clear the Americans from the river. On October 22, 1777, Colonel Carl Von Donop and about 1,200 Hessians attacked Fort Mercer. The Hessians were driven back, suffering 500 or more causalities including their commander, while American causalities were light. Many of the wounded were taken to the Whitall house where they were tended by American doctors and Ann Whitall who had remained in her home. The home turned hospital, was built in 1748 as a two-and-a-half story Georgian-style brick house. It has a gable roof with chimneys at either end. The farmhouse is 40 feet wide and 35 feet deep. The stone wing of two stories was built sometime earlier, and contains the kitchen and three rooms. The Whitall family owned the 400-acre farm until 1862. The federal government bought the house in 1872; it is now owned by Gloucester County and is a house museum. The Red Bank Battlefield is a National Historic Landmark.

Nothnagle Log Cabin, (Gibbstown) Greenwich Township

It was a memorable day for the Rink family, owners of a seventeenth-century Swedish built log cabin, when Queen Silvia of Sweden visited in April 1988. She was touring South Jersey as part of celebrations marking the 350th anniversary of the founding of New Sweden in 1638. The Nothnagle cabin has been called the oldest log cabin in the United States. It is one of the few remaining log cabins that were once prevalent in the lower Delaware Valley following the settlement there of Swedes and Finns. The Nominating Petition said of the cabin: "The full dovetailing at the corners is a detail considered by some authorities to be of Finnish origin and is certainly early. The one room plan with a corner fireplace, the so-called Swedish plan, is also typical feature of many of the earliest domestic structures in the area. Although there are a number of seventeenth-century log cabins in the area, this example of the earliest plan and structure is extremely rare and perhaps unique." It was built between 1638 to 1643. The house is one story, measuring 16 by 20 feet, with a gable roof. It has a sleeping loft; the attached structure was added in the nineteenth century and does not impinge on the original log cabin. It was called Nothnagle after an early owner with a German surname. It was log cabins like this one brought to New Jersey and the Delaware Valley by Swedes and Finns that came to be called the American log cabin, which became part of the mythology of the frontier and westward migration. The house is owned by Doris and Harry Rink and open to visitors. It is in good condition and is not lived in.

Bodo Otto House, (Mickleton) East Greenwich Township

Dr. Bodo Otto was a noted surgeon, legislator, judge, and militia colonel. He also served as a physician for General Washington's Flying Camp, a reserve military force based in Perth Amboy that could be rushed to any engagement to provide reinforcements. The U.S. Army Reserve traces its beginnings to the Flying Camp, while the National Guard traces its heritage to the colonial militias. Dr. Otto was the senior physician in charge of hospitals at Valley Forge. After the war he was appointed a judge. His attractive Georgian-style stone house is two-and –a-half stories, with the front of finished stone and the other three sides of fieldstone. The entrance door leads into the living room; to the right is a parlor, with a kitchen behind it. The parlor and kitchen each have a fireplace that shares a common chimney. The second floor is a central hall plan with three bedrooms. The owner of the house, Bodo Otto, was born in Germany in 1748 and came to America with his family in 1755. They initially lived in Philadelphia and then moved to Swedesboro, NJ. Otto trained to be a doctor at the Philadelphia Medical Hospital. He married and moved to Mickleton in 1772. The house is privately owned.

Seven Stars Tavern, Woodstown

New Jersey's first drive-in featured a small service window (see insert) where coachmen or horsemen could ride up and get a beer or ale without dismounting. Drinks to go were cheaper than inside the tavern. Peter Lauterbach built the brick two-and-a-half story building as a tavern in 1762 to replace an earlier 1740s structure that was also called Seven Stars Tavern. On the left or southern gable note the patterned bricks with date 1762 and the initials of Peter and his wife Elizabeth Lauterbach. The original building is the two-and-a-half story core, the wing was added at an unspecified later date. The interior of the tavern was designed as a center hall with the bar on one side and two parlors on the other side. The main barroom had a corner bar, dining area, and a large fireplace. The second floor had five rooms. The tavern also had a hollow metal tube running from the bar to the second floor where patrons could yell their orders down to the bar. The tavern passed to Lauterbach's son, John, who was a staunch patriot during the Revolutionary War. Local tradition has it that he supplied the American army with much food and drink, and because of this the British raided the tavern in 1778. The tavern was one of the most celebrated in New Jersey and was a popular stop off on the stage route to Philadelphia. It was converted to a house in 1805 and has been used as a residence ever since, reversing the usual practice of turning a residence into a tavern. It is privately owned.

Dickinson House, Alloway Township

The highly decorative gable end of the Dickinson House makes it the best known of Salem County's approximately 37 patterned brick houses that were built in the early eighteenth century. Nowhere else in America has the number and detailed designs as the houses in Salem County, although there are a few in Cumberland and Burlington counties. The intricate designs are created by using vitrified or glazed bricks set in generally four different patterns: checkerboard, diamonds or vertical zigzags, and a combination of dates, initials, and designs in the gable end of a house. The builders of these houses were skilled bricklayers who settled in Salem between 1720–1764, migrating from eastern England. Local masons probably copied the work of a few skilled artisan immigrants thus spreading the patterned brick design style. Patterned brickwork was widely used in France and England during the sixteenth century. In England patterned brickwork was used for major buildings and then filtered down to vernacular architecture. The Dickinson House is brick, two-and-a-half stories, with a small-pent roof between the first and second floors. The house measures 20 feet deep by 34 feet wide and there are large chimneys at either end of the house. The south gable has the intricate designs and marking I.M.D, 1754, which indicates owner and date of construction. It was built in 1754 by John and Mary Dickinson. John was a direct descendent of John Fenwick, the Quaker founder of Salem. The house has changed hands many times over the years, although the exterior core remains true to its original construction. The house is privately owned.

Wistarburgh Glassworks, Alloway Township

The first commercially successful glass factory in America was created in Salem County by Caspar Wistar in 1739, known as Wistarburgh Glass Manufactory, specializing in bottles and windowpanes. Glassmaking existed in Salem, Cumberland, and Gloucester counties because of rich silica sand, abundant wood fuel, and navigable waterways to deliver finished products. Upper left site of Wistarburgh Glassworks; upper right, bottle with Caspar's son Richard Wistar's emblem; lower left, Fairfield Presbyterian Church window panes made by Wistar; lower right, Colonial glass making.

Abel & Mary Nicholson House, Elsinboro Township

The Abel and Mary Nicholson house is a National Historic Landmark. It is considered one of the most significant early American homes in the United States. It is an outstanding example of Salem County's patterned brick houses. It was built in 1722, with elaborate, intact patterned brick designs on three exterior walls. The original house is in excellent condition and looks as it did when it was built. The 1722 core building is two-and-a-half stories, measuring approximately 36 feet wide by 22 feet deep, and has a gable roof, with chimneys at both ends. The house has never had electricity or central heating leaving the interior in original condition. The front door opens directly into a hall dominated by a fireplace; the other room is a parlor with an enclosed stairway. A Jersey Winder staircase leads to two rooms on the second floor, and above that is an unfinished attic. The house had a two-and-a-half story addition in 1859. The Landmark designation said of the house: "Fairbanks House, Bacon's Castle, and Drayton Hall represent an early period of construction in the New England Region, the Virginia Tidewater Region, and the Southern Region, respectively. The Abel and Mary Nicholson House has the potential of filing this early construction gap for the mid-Atlantic region by representing a building style (patterned brickwork) that in...New Jersey reached a higher state of elaboration and acceptance than anywhere else in America." The Samuel Nicholson family arrived in New Salem in 1675 from Nottinghamshire, England. The house was built for Samuel's youngest son, Abel. The family owned the property until 1852. It is in an isolated area of wetlands and is accessible by a one-half-mile, tick-infested dirt road. It is owned by Public Service Electric & Gas Co.

Ye Olde Centerton Inn, Pittsgrove

The Centerton Inn, New Jersey's oldest tavern was built in 1706, county deeds show. It is still operating as a restaurant and bar. Not much is known of the Inn's early history. It was owned by Charles Dayton in 1763 who had a license to operate a tavern at his home. The house was a stop on the stagecoach route from Greenwich to Philadelphia. It is said that during the Revolutionary War Marquess de Lafayette frequented the Inn. It is a wooden frame, two-and-a-half story building covered in clapboard, with gable roof, and two dormers. A Huffington Post website listing the 14 oldest taverns in the United States, listed Longfellow's Wayside Inn of Sudbury, Massachusetts as the oldest tavern, founded in 1716, not even close to the Centerton Inn's founding in 1706. But in all things Colonial and Revolutionary War Massachusetts and Virginia usually claim more than the facts warrant. The town where the Inn is located has undergone a number of name changes, beginning as Dayton's Bridge, then Centreville, and finally to Centerton.

Jones Law Office, Salem City

The John Jones Law Office is the oldest law office building in the United States, according to HABS. It was built about 1735 for one of Salem County's earliest attorneys. It is a one story, small octagon-shaped brick building, with a pyramid-like wooden shingle roof. The brickwork is laid in Flemish bond. Inside, the one room has plaster walls and a vaulted ceiling. This early example of an office building looks like a small Roman or Greek temple. Jones had his office here until he died in 1746. After that. Dr. Ebenezer Howell conducted his medical practice here. An office building, according to HABS is "… basically an attempt to separate family life from work, that is creating a private space." Offices started as single rooms in house, such as a parsonage, where the minister wrote his sermons—generally that room was called a study—away from family distractions. Doctors and lawyers were other early users of separate rooms in their homes for work. Study and library in Colonial or early American usage usually meant office. "Offices are designed for self-presentation. There can be no ramshackle or vernacular offices buildings, a handsome building denotes dependable service," HABS said. The Jones law office was moved in 1962, see insert, to its present location in a rear courtyard of the Grant House, which is headquarters for the Salem County Historical Society.

Alexander Grant House, Salem City

This house is a significant example of patterned brickwork. Not all patterned brickwork featured extensive gable end designs and the Grant House is typical of early Salem County architecture. The original brick section of two-and-a-half stories, with a gable roof and two dormers was built in 1721. There is a pent roof between the first and second story. Pent roofs are small roofs with a single slant. They were added to Georgian buildings to provide color and visual interest to otherwise dull solid stone or brick facades. The pent roof originated in Germany's Rhine River Valley where it was installed in houses above first story windows to protect exterior walls of half-timbered houses. German immigrants to Philadelphia used pent roofs in their houses even though they were no longer necessary to protect exterior walls. English neighbors adopted this building design and it spread throughout Pennsylvania and southern New Jersey, and somewhat to the other Middle Colonies. Alexander Grant, owner of the house, was from the county of Somerset in England, arriving in Salem about 1700. He was one of the founders of the Salem Episcopal Church in 1716 and was also a judge in Salem County courts. The original building was joined with two others to form the present façade. In the mid-1800s the buildings housed a temperance hotel, medical and law offices. John S. Rock the first African-American attorney admitted to practice law before the U.S. Supreme Court began his professional studies prior to 1850 here, an historic marker in front of the building said. The house was owned by the Grant Family until in 1921, when it was bequeathed to the Salem County Historical Society.

Friends Meetinghouse, Salem City

The Friends Meetinghouse is the oldest house of worship in Salem City, built in 1772 by William and Isaac Oakford on a design of William Ellis. It was the third Quaker meetinghouse in Salem; two earlier ones were at different locations. The first Quaker meeting was held at the home of Samuel Nicholson in 1681. Nicholson donated 16 acres for a cemetery and church site, near the famous Salem Oak tree. The austere rectangular Quaker meetinghouse, brick with gable roof, (see drawing) had the date of its construction in patterned brickwork. Many of the South Jersey meetinghouses are nearly identical. "Although the early Friends probably had no intention of creating a distinct type when they planned their places of worship, once that type was clearly defined and had become hallowed by tradition, they clung to it with characteristic tenacity." (Wartenbaker, p. 240). John Fenwick founded Salem when he bought land from the West Jersey Proprietors in 1675, creating what was originally called Fenwick's Colony. Two years later, Quakers founded Burlington farther up the Delaware River near Philadelphia. Fenwick was born in 1618 into a wealthy and influential family from Northumberland in England. In 1665 he became a Quaker, a religious group that was only founded in 1650 by dissident Puritans who were trying to reconcile Puritan spirituality with the reality of life. In England, George Fox was an early and defining leader of the Society of Friends.

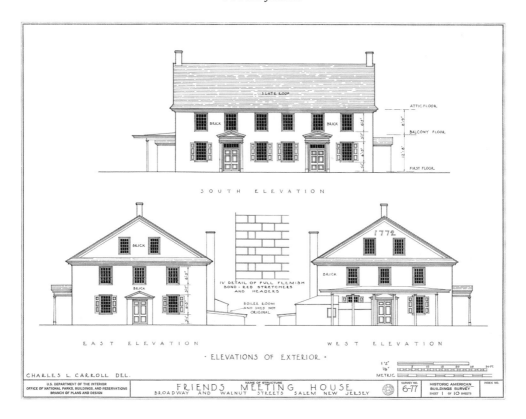

SLATE ROOF

ATTIC FLOOR

BALCONY FLOOR

BRICK   BRICK

FIRST FLOOR

S O U T H   E L E V A T I O N

BRICK   1772

BRICK   BRICK

1½" DETAIL OF FULL FLEMISH
BOND - RED STRETCHERS
AND HEADERS

BRICK   BOILER ROOM
BRICK   AND SHED NOT
ORIGINAL

E A S T   E L E V A T I O N   W E S T   E L E V A T I O N

· ELEVATIONS OF EXTERIOR ·

CHARLES L. CARROLL DEL.

U.S. DEPARTMENT OF THE INTERIOR
OFFICE OF NATIONAL PARKS, BUILDINGS AND RESERVATIONS
BRANCH OF PLANS AND DESIGN

NAME OF STRUCTURE
FRIENDS   MEETING   HOUSE
BROADWAY AND WALNUT STREETS   SALEM NEW JERSEY

SURVEY NO.
6-77

HISTORIC AMERICAN
BUILDINGS SURVEY
SHEET 1 OF 10 SHEETS

INDEX NO.

*Salem Meetinghouse & Oak

The drawing shows different perspectives on the Salem Meetinghouse, built in 1772, as the gable-end date shows. The oak tree standing in the Quaker cemetery is part of the 16 acres Samuel Nicholson donated to the Quakers; it is about half-a-mile from the meetinghouse. Under the oak tree is where Fenwick signed a land purchase agreement with local Native Americans. The tree is more than 500 years old; a sign warns of falling limbs.

Emanuel Evangelical Lutheran Church, Friesburg

The Lutheran Church was built in 1768, replacing a wooden frame church that was built in 1738 to minister to a small German community. The Germans arrived here in the late 1730s and early 1740s to work at the nearby Wistarburg Glassworks (see page 103). The community grew up near the church. The glassworks owner, Casper Wistar, was born in the Palatinate region of Germany. He founded the glassworks in 1739. After he died in 1752 his son Richard took over the glassworks and maintained the practice of importing skilled German glassblowers to work at the glass factory. The attractive vernacular, mostly Georgian style brick church is two stories, with its façade in Flemish bond, with common bond brickwork on the other three sides. The circular window high above the paneled door served as a model for a number of other meetinghouse-style churches in Salem County. The Greek Revival gable end was added in an 1888 modernization. There is some controversy whether Jacob Fries, the founder of the community, was from Hesse, Germany or Friesland, a region of the Netherlands with its own distinct language, Frisian, a Germanic language that became the basis for the original form of English. The church is situated at a crossroads in a rural farming community, much as it was 250 years ago.

Deerfield Presbyterian Church, Deerfield

One of the most attractive churches in New Jersey, the Deerfield Presbyterian Church was built in 1771 and has been in continuous use since then. The sandstone building has evolved over the years reflecting changes in Presbyterian theology and also how a church should look. When it was built it looked very much like the Fairfield Presbyterian Church (page 112). Alterations in 1858 and 1907 included rounded and arched windows, entrance tower and belfry, and internal arrangement of pews to modernize the church.

Fairfield Presbyterian Church, Fairfield

A pristine example of an early Presbyterian Church built in 1780, in a Georgian meetinghouse style. The building on the previous page, shows how most meetinghouse style churches, except the Quakers, evolved. Stones for the church, just like at Deerfield Church, were gathered by farmers from their fields to make the two-story building. Inside, pews and woodwork, are exactly as originally built; a number of original glass window panes were made by Witsarburgh Glassworks. The church is not in use.

Potter's Tavern, Bridgeton

Considered home of New Jersey's first newspaper, the tavern was built about 1740. At Christmas 1775, local patriots published a hand-written newspaper called the *Plain Dealer* calling for independence. Richard Howell and Joseph Bloomfield, both of whom later became governors of New Jersey, wrote articles for the fledging newspaper that Potter displayed at his tavern. The building is wooden frame, two-and-half stories modified Saltbox, sheathed in clapboard. Inside, the tavern was a central hall and parlor configuration.

Gibbon House, Greenwich

The Gibbon house is considered an excellent example of early Georgian architecture in New Jersey. It was built in 1730, modeled after a London Townhouse, and is two-and-a-half-story checkered, patterned brick. The steep-pitch roof has three dormers and interior chimneys at the gable ends. Inside, an entry hall with an open stairway leads to the second floor. On the ground floor there are large rooms on either side of the hall (see drawing), and at the end of the hall is a large kitchen.

The home's owner, Nicholas Gibbon, lived in Greenwich from 1730 to 1740. At that time Greenwich was a growing port, part of John Fenwick's original land grant. It was named after Greenwich in London. Nicholas Gibbon moved to Salem into what is now the Alexander Grant house, Gibbons and Grants intermarried. Nicholas was appointed Salem County sheriff in 1741 and was appointed county clerk in 1748.

His brother Leonard stayed behind in Greenwich running a family store. Nicholas Gibbon and his brother Leonard came to Salem and Cumberland counties from Bennesdere, England. The Greenwich house is headquarters for the Cumberland County Historical Society.

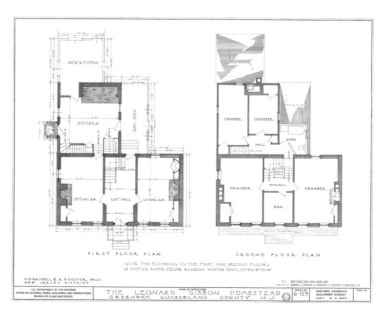

Swedish Granary, Greenwich

Said to be the oldest agricultural building in America, the Swedish granary was built between 1650–1660 in Hopewell Township. It was moved to Greenwich in 1976. A granary was an outbuilding designed to store grains, like wheat and other cereal crops, in bags or purpose-built bins. Threshing of grain took place on packed earth in front of the granary or in a barn and moved to the granary. The one-story log building was enclosed on three sides by cedar logs laid in notched and crossed corners, the fourth side is lattice work to allow air circulation. The one-story building was split horizontally with the top section open as a hayloft for loose hay, the ground floor section held bags of grain. The roof has a fairly steep pitch and the gable ends were made of vertical boards. The Nominating Petition said: "Mr. and Mrs. Carl Lindborg of Newton Square, Pennsylvania, known as authorities on the Swedish experience in the Delaware Valley said the log structure is the sole surviving example of this type of building from earliest European settlement in the region and is absolutely unique."

Richard Wood Store, Greenwich

The Richard Wood Store, built in 1773, looks like the day it first opened except for adding electricity and plumbing. It is a one story, wooden-frame building, sided in clapboard, with an attic and gable ends. It was built over a stone foundation. At the time of a 1936 HABS study the store was still in operation. It had been built by the first proprietor, Richard Wood 3rd, who was born in Greenwich February 7, 1755. Richard 3rd started his career as a schoolteacher but opened a store with two partners, eventually buying them out. He ran a successful general store and was also a farmer and cooper. He found time to represent Cumberland County in the New Jersey legislature. He was the son of well-known Quaker, Richard Wood, who bought the Gibbon house on then Main Street in 1759. The house stayed in the family until 1934. Richard Wood senior was a judge in the Cumberland County Court of Common Pleas. His father came from Bristol, England in 1682 settling in Philadelphia, until moving to Greenwich. The store is privately owned.

Caesar Hoskins Log Cabin, Mauricetown

The Caesar Hoskins Swedish log cabin dates to at least 1714 and possibly to 1680.

The Nominating Petition said: "The quality of the architecture is a fine example of early techniques used by the Swedes who first settled in South Jersey. The cabin is constructed of four inch by thirteen inch cedar logs (thick planks) ... the logs are joined in full dovetailed fashion and Swedish "V" joint extending the entire length of the logs. The logs are numbered using a primitive technique known to have been practiced in Sweden, that is: ' III' for 8 inches. The cabin is about 16 feet deep by 20 feet wide. The logs are well preserved because they were covered in lathe and plaster for more than 100 years. The logs, floor joists, ceiling beams, roof rafters, and the floorboards of the second floor are original. One of the original interior beams has a Swedish schooner carved into it, a one-of-a kind discovery in any New World Swedish settlements. The windows and door have been replaced. An addition was made to the east side of the house in the 1800s for a first floor kitchen and dining room, with bedrooms on the second floor. The house is named after a subsequent owner Caesar Hoskins, who first came to the Mauricetown area in 1691 as a whaler. He immigrated to the United States from Bristol, England in 1684. He lived in the house until 1724. It is privately owned.

Governor Howell Plantation, Shiloh

The house has two claims to fame. It was the home of Richard Howell who became the third governor of New Jersey and for William Howell, whose daughter, Varina Howell, became the wife of Confederate President Jefferson Davis. The house was built about 1770 and initially owned by two brothers, Lewis and Richard Howell. The house is a two-story brick structure with a gambrel roof, and a one- and –a- half story brick wing. The Howell family, farmers and devout Quakers, emigrated from Wales to Delaware about 1724, and at an unknown date moved to New Jersey. Richard Howell was born in 1754. He was educated at a local academy and at home, and eventually became an attorney. He was active in anti-British activities, including participating in the Greenwich Tea Party and also writing articles calling for independence in the *Plain Dealer*, the newspaper published at Potter's Tavern in nearby Bridgeton. He served as an infantry Major during the Revolutionary War and during the war converted to Episcopalism. He fought in the battles of Brandywine, Germantown, and Monmouth. He was at the Valley Forge encampment during the winter of 1777–1778; he resigned his commission while there to perform intelligence work for Washington. After the war, he practiced law in Trenton and was named a clerk to the State Supreme Court. He was an early member of the Federalist Party, the party of George Washington and Alexander Hamilton. Howell served as governor of New Jersey from 1793 to 1801. He and his wife Keziah had nine children, including William whose daughter Varina would become the wife of Confederate President Jefferson Davis.

Franklin Inn, Port Republic

The Franklin Inn was built in the 1750s, overlooking Nacote Creek near the mouth of the Mullica River. The oldest section, a two story wood frame structure, with gable roof and covered by clapboards, was the original tavern. The brick section was built in 1815 and served as a store and post office. The tavern and store were joined together in the 1920s creating a single façade as the owners turned the commercial property into a private residence. In the late eighteenth century, the tavern was owned by Sea Captain Macaja Smith whose daughter and son-in-law operated it. The Franklin Inn was on the stagecoach route between Chestnut Neck and Clark's Mill, two Atlantic County settlements. The Inn may have been named after New Jersey Royal Governor William Franklin. who apparently frequented the place. The town of Port Republic, where the inn is situated, was established in the mid-eighteenth century as a mill site. During the late eighteenth and through the nineteenth centuries Port Republic was a busy industrial and shipbuilding center and active port connecting into Mullica River, which leads into Great Bay and then into the Atlantic Ocean. The house is privately owned.

Risley Homestead, Northfield Township

The house is a reminder of and testimonial to the centuries the Atlantic Ocean and Delaware Bay and its bounty provided a living for generations of people clamming, fishing, cultivating, and dredging for oysters. The house was built in approximately 1780 by Edward Risley, an oysterman, whose family lived in the house until 1988, when it was donated to the Atlantic County Historical Society. Like most settlers along the southern New Jersey shore, the Risleys were from New England, specifically Hartford, Connecticut. Jeremiah Risley married a woman from New Jersey and by 1724 he owned land in the vicinity of the present house. His son Edward built the house, which the Nominating Petition described, as "The original core of the house is an example of simple vernacular architecture in southern coastal New Jersey in the eighteenth century. The timber framing, with heavy tapered corner posts and board-sheathed rafters shows some New England influence. The plan, however, with gable end chimneys and lacking hall or entry is a type commonly found in the Middle Colonies and may reflect some influence from the Delaware Basin, the prime market for South Jersey's maritime resources." Like buildings in northern New Jersey that show both Dutch and English influence, houses in South Jersey were also built showing different building traditions.

Somers Mansion, Somers Point

The Somers Mansion, a house really, was built in 1725 on a bluff overlooking Great Egg Harbor. The house is the oldest building in Atlantic County. It is brick, laid in Flemish bond, of two-and-a-half stories with a gambrel roof. It was expanded in 1760 and again in the late nineteenth century with the addition of second floor wrap around porch and a rear lean-to. The porches were removed as a WPA project in the 1930s to restore the house to its eighteenth century look. Inside there are two rooms on each floor, connected by a Jersey Winder staircase. The Somers were a prominent South Jersey family who migrated, initially, to Philadelphia in 1681 from Worcester, England, with a group of other Quakers. They moved to West Jersey in 1695. John Somers, the patriarch, bought 3,000 acres of land, including the house site, from Thomas Budd, one of the original West Jersey Proprietors. His descendants, all named Richard, I, II, & III, played important roles in New Jersey history. Richard II was a colonel in the Egg Harbor Militia and later was a judge. Richard III was a naval hero in the Battle of Tripoli as commander of the *Nautilus;* he was killed in the battle in 1804. The family owned the house until 1937 when it was deeded to Atlantic County. The state took over the property in 1941 as an historic site.

Friends Meetinghouse, Seaville

The cottage-like building is easily missed in its setting on busy Route 9 in upper Cape May County. The one room, one story, wooden frame, clapboard covered building was erected in 1763 as the Seaville Friends Meetinghouse. Because of its small size, 24 feet wide by approximately 20 feet deep, many people mistakenly believe it was built much earlier. The date usually given for its construction is 1727. That date was probably "based on a minute of the Great Egg Harbor and Cape May Monthly Meeting, Dated 3rd mo. 29th, 1727...it is concluded to build a Meetinghouse by Jacob Garretson's who is to give one acre of land for the service of said meeting. . .That citation most certainly referred to the meetinghouse at Beesley's Point" (Tvaryanas, unpaginated). It was also reported that the meetinghouse at Beesley's Point had been removed to Seaville. "This is also unlikely."(Tvaryanas, unpaginated). Incidentally, why members of the Society of Friends are called Quakers has several stories citing the reason. Essentially, it means, "quaking before the Lord." Some sources said King George used the word in complaining about members of the Society of Friends. Other sources said it was a judge in the trial of George Fox who uttered the phrase. Regardless, it has an English source and was used before the Quakers moved to America.

John Holmes House, Cape May Courthouse

John Cresse, a carpenter, built the initial house on this site in 1704. His father, Arthur Cresse a whaler from Long Island, bought about 350 acres of land from the West Jersey Society in 1695.

Arthur in turn sold to his son John about 150 acres the same year the house was built. The original house was two-stories with one room on each level. In the photograph the original house is the left side, with a larger 1804 addition attached to it. The wooden frame house had clapboard siding and gable end chimney. It was approximately 20 feet wide by 18 feet deep. The first floor kitchen is in the original building. The house stayed in the Cresse family until 1776 when it was sold to John Holmes, whose family lived in the house until 1935. The house is considered a good example of vernacular Georgian architecture with its detailed woodwork. The Cape May Historical & Genealogical Society bought the building in 1976 for its headquarters and museum.

Carman-Norton House. Lower Township

The Carman-Norton House, built between 1690 and 1722, is located at the intersection of Ferry and Seashore roads in the Cold Spring section of Cape May County, where two historic colonial houses are across the street from each other. The other house is Aaron Eldredge House (1760). The oldest part of the Carman-Norton House is the door and the windows to the left side in the photograph. The house was 24 feet wide by approximately 16 feet deep of wood frame construction sided with clapboards. The initial house was two rooms, one on each floor connected by a Jersey Winder staircase. Caleb Carman of the Carman-Norton house came to Cold Spring in 1688 from Long Island. He was both a whaler and a miller. He sold the house to Nathaniel Norton in 1716, who enlarged the house to its present dimensions in about 1722. A side lean-to was added to the house in the early 1800s. The house is an excellent example of vernacular Georgian architecture and has been featured in *Early American Life* magazine.

Memucan Hughes House, Cape May City

The Memucan Hughes House, built about 1761, seems out of place among the Victorian splendor of Cape May. Few visitors who come to admire the various forms of Victorian-era architecture, Queen Ann, Second Empire, Richardson Romantic, Gothic Revival and more, stop to think why Cape May City has almost exclusively Victorian-era architecture. The answer is one word: Fire. Cape May is the nation's oldest coastal resort and was still a popular destination when on November 8, 1878, fire engulfed the city and raged for 11 hours destroying its downtown commercial and residential areas. The town rebuilt more than 600 summer homes, hotels, and commercial structures in the then popular Victorian styles, creating today's Mecca of nineteenth-century framed buildings. As more coastal resorts opened, and rail routes bypassed Cape May, the town withered as a tourist destination and became a backwater fishing port, thus preserving its Victorian architecture from developers. A revival of interest in Victorian-era architecture in the 1970s spurred resurgence in tourism that continues today. The Hughes house, one of just a couple of Colonial houses left standing in Cape May City, was built by Memucan, grandson of a Long Island whaler, who moved here in 1689. The two-story, wood frame clapboard covered house had a couple of unique features. Its layout of two rooms deep was unusual for its time period, and its center chimney, which served the two downstairs back-to-back rooms, a kitchen and parlor, simultaneously was also unusual. A Jersey Winder staircase leads to the second floor with one large bedroom and two smaller ones. It is believed Memucan ran an illegal tavern in his house because he was cited in 1799 for "causing a public nuisance." The house is owned by the Greater Cape May Historical Society.

Bibliography

Bastien, Lynn, Jan. *Ghosts of Mount Holly.* Charleston: The History Press, 2008.

Boyer, S., Charles. *Old Inns and Taverns in West Jersey.* Camden: Camden New Jersey Historical Society, 1962.

_____ *Early Forges and Furnaces in New Jersey.* Philadelphia: University of Pennsylvania, 1931.

Brush, E., John. *The Population of New Jersey.* New Brunswick: Rutgers University Press, 1956.

Cooley, Scofield, Henry. *A Study of Slavery in New Jersey.* Baltimore: Johns Hopkins University Press, 1896. Also available as an e-book.

Foster, Gerald. *American Houses: A Field Guide To The Architecture Of The Home.* New York: Houghton Mifflin, 2004.

Greenagel, L., Frank. *The New Jersey Churchscape: Encountering 18th –and 19th Century Churches.* New Brunswick: Rutgers University Press, 2001.

Historic American Building Survey. Library of Congress, Prints & Photographs Division, Washington DC. www.loc.gov/pictures/collection/hh/

Mellick, Jr. Andrew D. *Story of An Old Farm.* New Brunswick: Rutgers University Press, 1948.

National Register of Historic Places, National Park Service, Washington, DC. *To get the file National Register's website: www.cr.nps.gov./nr*

New Jersey Department of Environmental Protection, New Jersey's and National Register of Historic Places website: www.nj.gov/dep/hpo/1identify/nrsr_lists.htm.

New Jersey Inventory of Historic Places. Trenton: Department of Environmental Protection, Historic Preservation Office, reports and typescripts indexed by municipality. Various dates. No website for this material.

Tavernor, Robert. *Palladio and Palladianism.* London: Thames & Hudson, 1991.

Tvaryanas, Damon. *The New Jersey Quaker Meetinghouse: a Typology and Inventory.* (Philadelphia: University of Pennsylvania, Master's Thesis, 1993)

Wacker, O., Peter. *Land and People: A Cultural Geography of Preindustrial New Jersey: Origins and Settlement Patterns.* New Brunswick: Rutgers University Press, 1975.

Wertenbaker, J., Thomas. *The Founding of the American Civilization: The Middle Colonies.* New York: Cooper Square Publishers, 1963.

Index

The buildings in the book are arranged geographically basically running north to south, and west to east, so it is relatively easy to find places by region using The Table of Contents. Below is a functional index listing buildings alphabetically by type.

Photo Credits

All color photographs are by David Veasey, except: page 103, the bottle with the seal of Richard Wistar, courtesy of the Corning Museum of Glass, Corning, NY.; window of Wistar-made panes and interior of Fairfield Church, courtesy of Michael Schuelke, pastor and photographer. All black and white photographs are by David Veasey except: page 12, St. Stephen Walbrook Church, Wren File, Wikipedia; page 95 and page 106 courtesy of National Register of Historic Places.